# BOND vs. BOND

## THE MANY FACES OF 007

### PAUL SIMPSON

Race Point
PUBLISHING

Quarto is the authority on a wide range of topics.

Quarto educates, entertains and enriches the lives of
our readers—enthusiasts and lovers of hands-on livir

www.quartoknows.com

First published in the United States of America in 2015 by
Race Point Publishing, a member of
Quarto Publishing Group USA Inc.
142 West 36th Street, 4th Floor
New York, NY 10018
Telephone: (212) 779-4972
Fax: (212) 779-6058
quartoknows.com
Visit our blogs at quartoknows.com

10 9 8 7 6 5 4 3 2 1

ISBN: 978-1-63106-000-7

Library of Congress Cataloging-in-Publication Data is available

Please see page 187 for the photography credits.

Cover illustration by Guy Stauber
Cover design by Heidi North
Interior design by Renato Stanisic
Text by Paul Simpson

Printed in China

For Barbara: Thanks for a wonderful decade.

*"The target of my books lay somewhere between the solar plexus and the upper thigh."*

–Ian Fleming, 1962

CONT

*ABOVE: Ian Fleming at his desk in Jamaica. LEFT: Sean Connery returns as Bond in Never Say Never Again. OPPOSITE TOP: Roger Moore in his early days of Bondage. OPPOSITE BOTTOM: Woody Allen as Jimmy Bond in the 1967 Casino Royale.*

ENTS

# INTRODUCTION

*"Bond, James Bond."*

**—initially said to Sylvia Trench in *Dr. No*—and then to many others subsequently.**

EVERYONE KNOWS WHO JAMES BOND IS: HE'S THAT SECRET AGENT FROM ENGLAND WE ALL RELY ON TO SAVE THE WORLD. LIKE GERRY ANDERSON'S PUPPET HERO CAPTAIN SCARLET, OR *DOCTOR WHO*'S CAPTAIN JACK HARKNESS, HE'S PRETTY MUCH INDESTRUCTIBLE—NO MATTER WHAT THE BAD GUYS THROW AT HIM, HE'LL SURVIVE WHAT NONE OF THE REST OF US WOULD HAVE A CHANCE OF LIVING THROUGH.

---

Except that isn't the character created by Ian Fleming over sixty years ago. The Bond we first meet, in *Casino Royale*, makes mistakes. He's fooled by agents working for "Redland" (i.e. Soviet Russia). He's brutally tortured and maimed. He takes uppers to keep himself going, and has an alcohol and nicotine intake that would horrify your friendly neighborhood doctor.

Is he even English? On screen, he's been portrayed by a Scot (Sean Connery), an Australian (George Lazenby), a Welshman (Timothy Dalton), and an Irishman (Pierce Brosnan)—and Fleming even made a few changes to Bond's own history to reflect Connery's performance.

**OPPOSITE:** *Sean Connery enjoys the view during a break in the shooting of* Thunderball's *bathtub scene with Luciana Paluzzi.*

That's where this book comes in. There are plenty of guides to 007 that tell you the history of the films, or the books, but the vast majority of them treat James Bond as a single figure—and he quite clearly isn't. There have been numerous official novels continuing the Bond legend—some written by high-profile authors, including Kingsley Amis, Sebastian Faulks, and William Boyd—and each writer has, consciously or unconsciously, brought his own version of 007 to the table. There was a long-running comic strip whose author openly admitted that he had toned down elements of Bond that he wasn't comfortable with. The movies themselves have adapted to suit the actor playing them: imagine putting Roger Moore's urbane characterization of 007 into the middle of *Licence to Kill*, or *Quantum of Solace*.

*Bond vs. Bond* will help you find the version of Bond that suits your own preferences, looking at the way 007 has been presented in the various media over the years, and placing that in the context of his creation. The other elements of Bond's world are also examined—from the guns to the girls, and the gadgets to the villains—to present a rounded view of all sides of the man who, no matter which incarnation you prefer, is undoubtedly the world's greatest secret agent.

# BOND
## *vs.* BOND

# CHAPTER 001

# THE LIFE OF IAN FLEMING

H E'S BEEN DESCRIBED AS "THE MAN WHO WOULD BE BOND," AND IT'S BEYOND DOUBT THAT WRITING THE 007 STORIES WAS A KIND OF WISH FULFILLMENT FOR IAN FLEMING, BUT— UNLESS THERE ARE SOME STILL-TO-BE-DECLASSIFIED DOCUMENTS WHICH INDICATE TO THE CONTRARY—THE AUTHOR OF THE JAMES BOND SERIES NEVER QUITE LIVED THE SORT OF LIFE HE DEVISED FOR HIS MOST FAMOUS CREATION.

Smoke, yes; drink to excess, yes; womanize, yes. Save England from the predations of diabolical masterminds, whether they were ex-Nazis or members of SMERSH and SPECTRE? No—although he would certainly have loved an opportunity to do so, and Fleming's high regard for those who engaged in such derring-do permeates at least the early books in the Bond canon.

Ian Lancaster Fleming was born on May 28, 1908, in Green Street, Mayfair, in London. His paternal grandfather, Robert, had traveled from Dundee to London in the late nineteenth century, after making a fortune through the Scottish American Investment Company, which he cofounded in 1873. Robert also established his own investment bank, Robert Fleming & Co., at the same time, which was extremely prosperous, allowing the Fleming family to buy land in Oxfordshire and maintain a house in Grosvenor Square, London.

*Pupils at Eton in their traditional school uniform—as James Bond would have worn when he attended the school.*

Robert had two sons, Valentine and Philip, and the former went on to become a successful barrister, marrying Evelyn Beatrice St. Croix Rose, the daughter of a London solicitor. They had four sons—Peter, Ian, Richard, and Michael—over the space of six years, during which time Valentine was elected Member of Parliament for Henley, Oxfordshire. In the years leading up to the outbreak of World War I, the family spent their time at Braziers Park, their home near Wallingford, Oxfordshire, and Pitt House on Hampstead Heath, north London. A house for the Flemings was also constructed at Arnisdale, near Kyle of Lochalsh in the Scottish Highlands.

By the time the Great War began in the summer of 1914, Ian was enrolled at a preparatory school in Dorset, which he did not enjoy; from there, he would follow in his father's footsteps and attend the prime public (fee-paying) school in the country, Eton. However, long before he started there in 1921, his father was killed in action with the Queen's Own Oxfordshire Hussars at Ypres on the Western Front in 1917, just one week before Ian's ninth birthday. Valentine's obituary was penned by future prime minister Winston Churchill.

Ian's time at Eton saw him awarded the prestigious Victor Ludorum ("Winner of Games") prize on two occasions, and his abilities at athletics outshone his academic gifts—the reverse of his older brother, Peter. His writing talents were developed during his editorship of a school magazine, *The Wyvern*, but his attitude to life meant that he was often in conflict with his housemaster, E.V. Slater, who particularly disapproved of Fleming's ownership of a car and relationships with women. Slater was able to persuade Evelyn Fleming to send Ian to a private tutor to prepare for the Royal Military College exam, but the army wasn't a good fit for Ian either.

In 1927, Ian started language studies at the Tennerhof in Kitzbühel, Austria, and later spent time at both Munich University and the University of Geneva. His passion for climbing and skiing also developed during these years—as did his fondness for women: he briefly became engaged to Monique Panchaud de Bottomes in 1931, but his mother disapproved, and Ian broke it off. He applied for entry to the Foreign Office, but failed the exam; after some judicious lobbying by his mother to Sir Roderick Jones, the head of Reuters News Agency, Ian was employed as a sub-editor and journalist in October 1931.

Although it was clear to Ian that a career at Reuters was not going to provide the sort of life that he wanted for himself, the time he spent there was very useful. He was sent by the agency to cover the trial of six engineers from the British company Metropolitan-Vickers in Moscow—a Stalinist show trial that opened Ian's eyes to the reality of life in the Communist state—and he even tried to get an interview with the leader of the USSR himself. Josef Stalin didn't accept the invitation, although he sent Ian a signed note of apology.

After his return from Moscow, Ian turned down the offer of a posting to Shanghai, and—after further pressure from his mother—went into finance, working at small financiers Cull & Co. before joining stockbrokers Rowe and Pitman in 1935. While he may not have shone at his new profession, he did find opportunities to improve his social life, and he spent time indulging in rounds of golf at the course at Sandwich in Kent (later the scene of the duel between Bond and Goldfinger), gambling at Le Touquet, or playing cards at various London clubs. His womanizing continued, with one of his conquests being Ann O'Neil, the wife of the 3rd Baron O'Neill—at the same time that she was involved with Esmond Harmsworth, son of the *Daily Mail*'s owner, Lord Rothermere.

## FLEMING GOES TO WAR

In May 1939, four months before the outbreak of World War II, Ian received a highly unusual job offer from Rear Admiral John Godfrey, the Director of Naval Intelligence in the British Royal Navy. Godfrey needed a personal assistant, and he felt Ian was the right person for the job—seeing something in the 31-year-old that others at the time, and subsequently, failed to spot. Ian was commissioned into the Royal Naval Volunteer Reserve in July 1939 as a lieutenant, but was quickly promoted to Commander after hostilities began on September 3. Codenamed 17F, Ian worked out of Room 39 at the Admiralty as Godfrey's liaison with many other government departments—eventually including the Secret Intelligence Service (the correct name for the department commonly known as MI6), the Joint Intelligence Committee, the Special Operations Executive, and the Political Warfare Executive. He also established many civilian contacts, and coordinated efforts with the code-breaking team at Bletchley Park.

Ian came up with many ideas for intelligence operations, including what was known as the "Trout Memo," which compared the necessity for deception of an enemy to the patience required in fly fishing. In 1940, Ian and Admiral Godfrey worked with Professor Kenneth Mason of Oxford University in preparing reports on the geography of the countries involved in the war; these reports eventually became the Naval Intelligence Division Geographical Handbook Series, which proved to be invaluable during the conflict. Ian also thought up a way to get hold of one of the German's Enigma codebooks; in Operation Ruthless, a captured German bomber would be manned by an English crew (suitably disguised as members of the Luftwaffe) and ditched in the English Channel. They would then overpower the Germans sent

*The codebreaking machines at the ultra-secret British facility at Bletchley Park.*

to rescue them, and bring their codebook back to Britain. However, this idea wasn't followed through.

Even before the United States entered the war in December 1941, Ian was liaising with Colonel "Wild Bill" Donovan, President Roosevelt's special representative for intelligence cooperation and the man who would come to be known as the "Father of American Intelligence." During one visit to America, Ian assisted with drafting the blueprint for the Office of the Coordinator of Information, which eventually became the Office of Strategic Services and then the Central Intelligence Agency. Shortly after that, Ian was placed in charge of Operation Goldeneye, a plan to maintain a spy network in Spain that could keep contact with agents in Gibraltar, should that fall to the Nazis, and to ensure that the Germans were not able to set up equipment in the Straits

*The living room at Goldeneye, the house that Ian Fleming had built in Jamaica, where he wrote the James Bond books.*

of Gibraltar that would be a threat to Allied shipping and the Navy's Mediterranean strategy. Ian traveled to Lisbon, Gibraltar, and Tangiers during the planning of Goldeneye, which took on more importance as Operation Torch, the Allied invasion of North Africa, unfolded. Goldeneye was closed down in August 1943 as the war effort proceeded in the Allies' favor.

What may have been Ian's greatest contribution to the war effort came in 1942—the creation of the No. 30 Commando unit, otherwise known as the 30 Assault Unit (30AU), a group of specialist troops who accompanied soldiers on raids with the specific purpose of obtaining intelligence. Ian was inspired by the work of a similar German group run by Otto Skorzeny, which had operated very successfully during the Battle of Crete in 1941. While Ian may not have fought alongside the group he referred to as his "Red Indians" in the field, he directed operations and selected their targets. Even after Admiral Godfrey was replaced as head of the Naval Intelligence Division by Edmund Rushbrooke, Ian's influence and control over 30AU continued, and the unit grew in size as its successes mounted up. It played a critical role in Operation Overlord, the Allied invasion of Europe, in 1944, and from December that year, Ian was posted to the Far East to scout out opportunities for the unit in the Pacific theater—although the surrender of Japan in August 1945 following the atomic bombs dropped on Hiroshima and Nagasaki by the United States meant that it didn't carry out many operations.

Ian had less day-to-day involvement with 30AU after June 1944, when he was sitting on the committee that selected targets for a unit known as T-Force (Target Force), whose job was to guard and secure documents, persons, and equipment, alongside combat and intelligence personnel, after large towns and ports were liberated from the enemy. T-Force had a notable success at the German port of Kiel, home to a key Nazi research center.

In 1942, Ian attended a conference in Jamaica and fell in love with the island. After the war ended in 1945, he purchased a plot of land with the help of his friend Ivar Bryce, and arranged construction of a house, named Goldeneye, which would become his home from home during the winter for the rest of his life.

## ENTER 007

Ian was demobbed in May 1945, immediately after the end of the war in Europe, and became foreign manager for the *Sunday Times*. His contract stated that he could take three months' holiday across the winter, and it was during these breaks that he wrote the novels that were to make him famous, all the while continuing to work for the paper. (His articles became the basis of his two non-fiction works: *The Diamond Smugglers* and *Thrilling Cities*.)

VINTAGE FLEMING

During the war, Ian had mentioned to various friends that he wanted to write a spy novel, and on February 17, 1952, he started work on *Casino Royale*—as a distraction, he later claimed, from his forthcoming wedding to Ann Charteris (the former Mrs. O'Neill), whom he had continued to see after the death of her first husband and her remarriage, to Esmond Harmsworth, the 2nd Viscount Rothermere. Ian and Ann's daughter Mary was stillborn in 1948, but Rothermere only divorced Ann in 1951. Ian and Ann married on March 24, 1952, five months before the birth of their son, Caspar, although the marriage was never a happy one, with both parties having affairs.

*The cover for the recent reprint of* Thrilling Cities, *a compilation of Fleming's guides to fourteen of the world's most exotic locations. It also includes a short Bond story: "007 in New York."*

Ian's friend William Plomer read the manuscript of *Casino Royale*, and sent a copy to Jonathan Cape, publishers of Ian's brother Peter's work. They released the book in April 1953, and it was an immediate success. Each winter Ian would write a new manuscript, which was published a year later, often drawing on his experiences during the war, and many of the people whom he worked with or knew of from that period. Although 007 might share elements of Ian's own life—his golf handicap, love of scrambled eggs (a recipe for which Ian provided in the comparatively unknown story "007 in New York," which appeared within *Thrilling Cities*), and even perhaps an idealized version of his own physicality—Bond scholars have seen aspects of the pre-war spy Conrad O'Brien-ffrench, one of the earliest agents working for the SIS; Patrick Dalzel-Job, one of 30AU's key operatives in the post-Overlord operations; and Wilfred Dunderdale, the SIS station chief in Paris, who wore handmade suits and was chauffeured around Paris in a Rolls-Royce.

*Live and Let Die, Moonraker, Diamonds Are Forever,* and *From Russia, with Love* appeared between 1954 and 1957 to general acclaim, but *Dr. No*'s publication in 1958 was greeted less favorably, following an article by Bernard Bergonzi in the magazine *Twentieth Century* which attacked the "strongly marked streak of voyeurism and sado-masochism" in the novels. Paul Johnson of the *New Statesman* called *Dr. No* "without doubt, the nastiest book I have ever read." Ian's

*Ian Fleming standing in front of the Orient Express on location for* From Russia with Love, *the second film based on his successful Bond novels.*

reaction to this wasn't immediately apparent—*Goldfinger*, the 1959 novel, had been written prior to the attacks—but he seemed to lose enthusiasm for 007. It didn't help that he and Ann were going through a particularly difficult bout of marital problems at the time.

Ian had hoped to see a screen version of his hero. *Casino Royale* had been adapted for American television (see pages 175–178) in 1954, but no series had followed. He worked on outlines for a potential television show, and used some of those in the book he wrote in 1959, *For Your Eyes Only*, a collection of five short stories. The next book, *Thunderball*, was also based on a script, but this time for a movie, *James Bond of the Secret Service*, on which Fleming had been working with Irish filmmaker Kevin McClory and screenwriter Jack Whittingham. Although the film project didn't proceed, Fleming's partners were incensed at Fleming's use of the story as the basis for the novel without their agreement, and a protracted court case followed, the ramifications of which would continue to be felt for the next half-century.

| *Ian Fleming and his wife Ann arrive for the London premiere of Dr. No.*

As someone who smoked and drank far more than his system could tolerate, Ian was always a candidate for heart problems, and he had a major heart attack in 1961. During his recuperation, he took the time to write down the children's story he had been telling his son Caspar; *Chitty-Chitty-Bang-Bang* (the book of which is considerably different to the later film) was the result, published shortly after his death. His "mainstream" Bond novel that year was the unusual *The Spy Who Loved Me*, an attempt to present his hero in a new way (see page 29); the experiment was deemed a failure.

Ian's reputation received a major boost around this time when new US President John F. Kennedy included *From Russia, with Love* in a list of his top-ten books. A few months later, in June 1961, Ian sold an option on the Bond rights to Canadian producer Harry Saltzman, who teamed up with Albert R. Broccoli to create EON Productions and produce the Bond series of films. Ian visited the sets of the first three—*Dr. No*, *From Russia with Love*, and *Goldfinger*—and Sean Connery's portrayal of 007 fed back into the books he was working on at the time.

Two further novels were published in Ian's lifetime: *On Her Majesty's Secret Service* and *You Only Live Twice*, both of which saw major changes in James Bond's fictional life. Ian completed a draft of *The Man with the Golden Gun* in the spring of 1964, although he wasn't happy with it. Soon after that, he was approached to write a spy series for television by American producer Norman Felton, and although Ian came up with characters called Napoleon Solo and April Dancer, he had nothing more to do with *The Man from U.N.C.L.E.* after EON asked him to withdraw to prevent a potential conflict of interest. (April Dancer later became the central character of *The Girl from U.N.C.L.E.* spin-off.)

On August 11, 1964, Ian suffered a heart attack at a hotel in Canterbury, and died early the following morning, aged 56. It was Caspar's twelfth birthday. British newspaper the *Guardian* noted his death, and commented in a leader that "even Bond, one imagines, can hardly survive his creator: 007 has bitten the dust at last." They couldn't have been wider of the mark . . .

# CHAPTER 002

# THE LITERARY BOND: IAN FLEMING'S 007

IAN FLEMING MIGHT HAVE THOUGHT OF JAMES BOND AS A "SILHOUETTE," A BLUNT INSTRUMENT WHOSE OUTLOOK ON LIFE WAS NOT PARTICULARLY OF INTEREST TO THE READER, BUT ACROSS THE COURSE OF THE NOVELS AND SHORT STORIES, WE LEARN A CONSIDERABLE AMOUNT ABOUT THE SECRET AGENT WITH THE LICENSE TO KILL.

## CASINO ROYALE

Bond's first appearance was in the novel *Casino Royale*, published in 1953. He's agent 007 in the British Secret Service, and is regarded as its finest gambler, hence his assignment to face Soviet agent Le Chiffre on the gaming tables at Royale-les-Eaux, where he also exposes Soviet double-agent Vesper Lynd.

He bears a certain resemblance to the singer Hoagy Carmichael, at least according to Vesper, who describes him as "very good-looking" (although Bond claims that he can't see the resemblance to Carmichael himself). He has gray-blue eyes, a short lock of black hair that constantly falls forward over his right eyebrow, and a thin vertical scar down his right cheek. Vesper comments that his handwriting is very clear and even

**OPPOSITE:** *Ian Fleming admires Richard Chopping's artwork on the cover of his latest novel, On Her Majesty's Secret Service.*
**ABOVE:** *The 1962 Pan UK edition of the first Bond book, the only version to depict the torture scene.*

A certain amount of Bond's past comes out during the story. He bought a 4½ Litre Bentley with a supercharger by Amherst Villiers nearly new in 1933, and worked with Deuxième Bureau agent René Mathis for two months on a case in Monte Carlo before World War II, watching two Romanians. He earned his "00" number—which means that he has had to kill in the course of his assignments—for two missions during the war: he killed a Japanese cipher expert in New York, shooting him from an adjoining building to the man's office in the Rockefeller Center, and a Norwegian double-agent in Stockholm, whom he had to kill with a knife in the man's bedroom. Toward the end of that conflict, he was stationed in Hong Kong, where he developed the habit of wearing a pajama-coat in bed. Since the end of hostilities, he has operated against the Soviet Union in various arenas, and was involved in a case in Jamaica.

Professionally, he doesn't have much time for women—he wonders why his superiors have sent him female agent Vesper Lynd, since he regards women as being "for recreation." He wants to sleep with Vesper, but only once the job is done—and believes that, because of her "central privacy," each time they have sex it will "have the sweet tang of rape." He has a dismissive attitude toward the process of seduction, normally adopting a "mixture of taciturnity and passion" to avoid the shame and hypocrisy of an affair. As the story progresses, however, he begins to fall under Vesper's spell, and is even considering proposing marriage to her. But then her treachery is revealed, and his cold, ruthless side reasserts itself—after he has dried his wet eyes. (Bond is sometimes accused of being a racist as well as a sexist, but it's worth noting that Fleming's stereotypical comments about French and Bulgarian people are not ascribed to Bond.)

He's a heavy smoker—around seventy a day of the special blend of Balkan and Turkish tobacco cigarettes created for him by Morlands of Grosvenor Street, London—and he takes a bachelor's pleasure in food and drink, being very particular about the way each is prepared. He enjoys a vodka martini, and has created his own very specific recipe for it, which he asks a bartender to use, recommending grain vodka rather than a spirit derived from potato. He originally decides to call it a "Vesper." He enjoys gambling, both at the roulette wheel and the card table, but knows never to "mistake bad play for bad luck"; he believes that he "only bets on even chances," and, as we learn in the first paragraphs of the book, he knows when to walk away from the table. He sleeps with his hand resting on a gun under his pillow—his own .38 Colt Police Positive with a sawn barrel—and uses a Beretta .25 the rest of the time.

At the end of the story, he is severely tortured by Le Chiffre, with a carpet beater forcibly applied to his genitals. His tolerance for pain is more than that of most people, but he is still incapacitated as a result. He is saved from death by the intervention of an agent from SMERSH, part of the Soviet spy apparatus, who carves the initial of the organization's name, the Cyrillic letter Ш (SCH), onto the back of his hand. The incident, however, makes him consider resigning from the service—although once he has recovered, this desire fades, with Vesper's death motivating him to take on SMERSH, exactly as Mathis predicts.

## LIVE AND LET DIE

Ian Fleming was already working on the second James Bond novel, *Live and Let Die*, before *Casino Royale* sold out its initial print runs. The second story was published in 1954, and saw Bond and his CIA ally Felix Leiter battle powerful black businessman Mr. Big, a member of SMERSH. The trail leads Bond from New York to Jamaica, where he and Solitaire, Big's voodoo-practicing telepathic fortune teller who has joined forces with him, are keelhauled almost to death, before a bomb destroys Big's boat, leaving the villain to the mercy of the sharks.

Bond hasn't been to America since the end of World War II, and he didn't spend any time in Harlem during his previous visit to New York. His assignment in Jamaica just after the war involved an attempt by the Cubans to infiltrate the labor unions, and while there he fell in love with the country and its people.

He has had a skin graft to cover the scar on his hand, taken from high up on his forearm, but nothing can be done about the scar on his face (even the FBI's "Cover-Mark" cannot mask it). He believes that there's a hint of the "mixed blood of America" in his hair and cheekbones, which will help with his cover—as do the military haircut he receives and the alterations to his wardrobe.

Although he was able to withstand the genital-beating doled out by Le Chiffre in *Casino Royale*, he faints from the pain when his little finger is broken. He is normally icy cold, but after Felix Leiter is nearly killed by a shark, blind rage overtakes him when he has the chance to get payback, and he kicks the man responsible into a shark tank. (Before he knows what his assignment is, he hopes that it's a chance to take revenge on SMERSH for what they did to him.) He is shaken by what he reads about voodoo practices, and,

*The 1973 Pan UK edition of the second novel, featuring the movie poster designed by Robert McGinnis for Roger Moore's debut.*

while in Jamaica, he whimpers and sweats in his sleep when dreaming of the deadly sea creatures he might encounter. He's slightly awestruck by both Mr. Big's physicality and his intelligence—he certainly doesn't look down on him. (Again, any racist or patronizing attitudes that may be displayed are authorial, rather than coming from Bond.)

His attitude to women while on assignment is changing: although he doesn't fully trust Solitaire when she asks to come with him from New York, he realizes he will have fun teasing her and being teased back during their train journey south. He has the self-control not to sleep with her, despite her coquettish behavior, keeping his desire for her in a "compartment which had no communicating door with his professional life." However, when they are both captured by Mr. Big, he coldly decides that he will drown her rather than let her be torn to pieces by the sharks. When they survive, M grants Bond "passionate leave."

While working, Bond is able to control his vices: after a week of training on Jamaica, he is down to ten cigarettes a day, and has not had an alcoholic drink. As a result of this—and the Benzedrine amphetamine tablets he takes—he is able to swim two miles easily. He still indulges his gourmand tastes when he can: he looks forward to drinking the best champagne in Jamaica when the mission is over, and he and Felix Leiter indulge themselves in New York.

## MOONRAKER

Bond's third appearance, in 1955, was in *Moonraker*, which pits him against Sir Hugo Drax, creator of a great rocket that, ostensibly, is going to put Britain ahead in the technological race. However, Drax is really a Nazi who intends to destroy London, and, in the end, only Bond and undercover police officer Gala Brand can stop him.

The story is set completely in the home counties of England in 1954, allowing Fleming to give us an insight into Bond's life when he's not globetrotting. He is the best shot in the Service, even if no one is going to tell him so. He earns £1,500 per year, and has £1,000 tax-free from private income, but while on assignment, he is allowed to spend freely. As an agent of the Secret Service, he usually cannot operate within the United Kingdom (a distinction between MI5, the domestic security agency, and MI6, the "foreign" or international service, for whom Bond would work in the real world). He shares a secretary, Loelia Ponsonby, with the other members of the

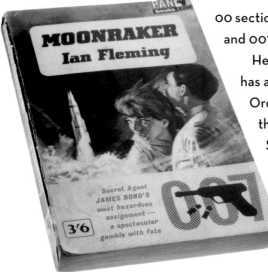

MOONRAKER
Ian Fleming

Secret Agent
JAMES BOND'S
most hazardous
assignment—
a spectacular
gamble with fate

3'6

*Gala Brand, on the cover of this 1962 Pan UK edition of Moonraker, is one of the Bond girls who never made it to the big screen.*

00 section—008 (Bill), who is on assignment in East Germany, and 0011, who has been "lost" in Singapore.

He is aged 37, and must retire from active duty at 45. He has already been awarded the CMG (Companion of the Order of St. Michael and St. George), but M turns down the offer of the George Cross on his behalf, since it is Service policy not to allow officers to accept such honors. His relationship with M rarely extends beyond the office, and it's unusual for M to call him "James."

Bond has never particularly liked moustaches, and does not know the names of wild flowers. While he was in Paris he visited the *maisons tolérées* (the legalized brothels). He was in Germany the year before *Moonraker*, and can speak fluent German. He learned his card-sharping skills from an American expert, Steffi Esposito, before the war, prior to the assignment in Monte Carlo watching the Romanians, and he brushes up on them before beating Sir Hugo at bridge. He knows little to nothing about rocketry, although he keeps abreast of current affairs—he is able to reel off Drax's life story with little prompting—and has a working knowledge of psychiatric conditions. He is prepared, if necessary, to give his life for his work, believing that lighting a last cigarette beneath the *Moonraker* tail will be the only way to stop the rocket destroying London.

When not on assignment, Bond works in the office on weekdays between 10 a.m. and 6 p.m., taking lunch in the canteen usually, and either playing cards in the evening or making love to one of three married women. At the weekends, he plays golf for high stakes. He still has his 1930 4½ Litre Bentley coupé, in which he carries a long-barreled .45 Colt Army Special in a concealed holster under the dash, but the car is wrecked during this operation, and replaced by a 1953 Mark VI Touring Bentley, paid for with his winnings from Drax. Bond once "dabbled on the fringe" of the motor-racing world.

His love of food is made clear—his breakfast regime, prepared by his Scottish housekeeper May in his flat off the King's Road in Chelsea, and the elaborate dinner that he consumes while dining with M at Blades club are detailed—and he enjoys good champagne and vodka, which he learned how to drink while stationed in Moscow. He takes more Benzedrine to keep his wits about him.

While on this assignment, he is attracted to Gala Brand, the undercover police officer, but this goes nowhere since, as he learns at the end of the story when he is about to make his move, she is engaged to be married. This allows Fleming, for a moment, to show the more melancholy and lonely side to Bond as he walks away from the young lovers.

## DIAMONDS ARE FOREVER

James Bond's next assignment was *Diamonds Are Forever*, first published in 1956, in which he follows a diamond pipeline into America and encounters the Spang brothers. He is hindered then helped by smuggler Tiffany Case.

Bond is still aged under 40, and has just returned from two weeks' leave in France. He's in "pretty good shape." He knows how to use a Bofors gun, and his unarmed combat is satisfactory—which we see demonstrated for one of the first times in the series in the fight in Spectreville. It doesn't do him any good when Seraffimo Spang decides to order him to suffer an "eighty-percenter" Brooklyn stamping, which he barely survives, and he hallucinates as he regains consciousness.

One of his earliest jobs for the Service was as a courier on various routes: through Strasbourg into Germany, through Niegoreloye into Russia, over the Simplon, and across the Pyrenees.

It's the first time we really see Bond showing any sense of humor when his mind turns to a double entendre that M has unwittingly made. His friendship with Felix Leiter brings out the best in Bond, although he's not impressed with the "style" of Las Vegas, dubbing it the "Gilded Mousetrap" school of architecture, nor with its gambling inhabitants, who are described in terms used nowadays for zombies. He recognizes the tune "Les Feuilles Mortes" (better known as "Autumn Leaves"), has "memories" connected to "La Vie en Rose," and read *Alice in Wonderland* many years earlier.

The book gives us the greatest insight since *Casino Royale* into Bond's view of women, in a conversation with Tiffany that comes not long after he's started to express a few doubts about his choice of profession to himself. He's never married because he thinks he can handle life better on his own. However, a perfect mate for him could make "Sauce Béarnaise as well as love," and he notes that although he wants children, it won't be possible until he retires. In fact, as he admits to Tiffany, he is effectively "married to a man named M." He does fall for her, though, seeing the damaged girl beneath the veneer of hardness.

# FROM RUSSIA, WITH LOVE

The fifth novel, *From Russia, with Love* (1957), was Fleming's first attempt at altering the successful formula, with the opening third of the book detailing a SMERSH plot against the British, and Bond in particular. A beautiful Russian girl, Tatiana Romanova, apparently has fallen in love with Bond's photo and wants to defect, together with a Spektor code device—as long as it's 007 who arranges it. Of course, it's a trap, and assassin Red Grant is ready to dispose of Bond as he travels on the Orient Express back from Turkey to England.

Bond came to the attention of SMERSH in 1946—or at least, that's the first photo they have of him on file, which shows his facial scar is three inches long. He is 183 centimeters (6 feet) tall and weighs 76 kilograms (168 lbs). He has another scar on his left shoulder. He is an expert pistol shot, boxer, and knife-thrower, and does not use disguises. He speaks French and German, smokes heavily, drinks—but not to excess—and women are regarded as one of his vices. He has a high tolerance of pain. Aged seventeen, he climbed the Aiguilles Rouges in the Alps, with companions from the University of Geneva. He has worked for the British Secret Service since 1938, and, for the first time, it is indicated that an "00" number means that he is "privileged to kill on active service." During that time, he has never worked in Turkey. He believes that the Service needs to employ intellectuals to deal with the challenges of modern spying. He doesn't believe in cyanide suicide pills, and gets rid of the one that Q Branch puts in his briefcase, which he uses to carry the other

*The 1963 Pan UK tie-in edition of the fifth novel had holes punched up the side to simulate the sprocket-holes on a film reel.*

tools of his trade, including his Beretta, a silencer, fifty rounds of ammunition, and two throwing knives.

He has not had an active mission for nearly a year, since *Diamonds Are Forever*. Tiffany moved in with him when they returned to the UK, but they argued and she left for America a month prior to the events in this book. He now sleeps naked (possibly Tiffany's influence—it's stated that American men prefer to do this), and tries to stay in shape with a rigorous morning exercise routine. He reads *The Times* and doesn't have a television set. As always, he is fastidious about his breakfast, with very specific preferences about the kind of eggs, jam, marmalade, and honey he has on wholewheat toast. When he is in a situation beyond his control, he goes into a mental "hurricane-room," which allows him to relax. He knows he is prejudiced about certain things—people who wear their ties in a Windsor knot, for example, are often cads—but he tries to overcome them.

He knows that he is effectively "pimping for England," and he is highly suspicious of Tatiana, the honey-trap proffered by SMERSH. However, he tries to live up to her expectations as a lover (his technique is described in more detail than previously). He knows that she is keeping something from him, despite passing him the Spektor that she had promised, and he doesn't make love to her on the Orient Express as they travel across Europe while there is still danger, although he is aware that her presence is making him let his guard down. He eventually admits to the head of Station T, Kerim Bey, with whom they are traveling, that he has fallen for her—but after Kerim is murdered, he reverts to his usual cold self for a time.

Unusually, Bond is gullible on two occasions with Soviet agents: firstly with "Nash" (the pseudonym Grant is using) on the Orient Express, believing his story, and then with Rosa Klebb, the head of SMERSH, when he encounters her in Paris. Despite his Beretta jamming, he captures the older woman, but she manages to get close enough to Bond to lash out with her poisoned-tipped boot . . .

## DR. NO

Although it seemed as if Fleming was trying to kill Bond off, he had already completed the next novel, *Dr. No*, before *From Russia, with Love* was published. Bond is sent to Jamaica on what should be an easy assignment, to investigate the

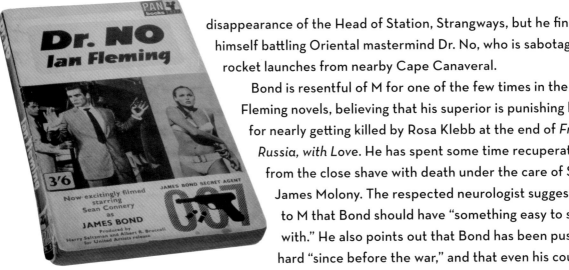

*Sean Connery, Jack Lord, and Ursula Andress in scenes from the new movie, Dr. No, on the cover of this Pan UK edition from 1962.*

disappearance of the Head of Station, Strangways, but he finds himself battling Oriental mastermind Dr. No, who is sabotaging rocket launches from nearby Cape Canaveral.

Bond is resentful of M for one of the few times in the Fleming novels, believing that his superior is punishing him for nearly getting killed by Rosa Klebb at the end of *From Russia, with Love*. He has spent some time recuperating from the close shave with death under the care of Sir James Molony. The respected neurologist suggests to M that Bond should have "something easy to start with." He also points out that Bond has been pushed hard "since before the war," and that even his courage might have its limits. However, Bond only enjoys the dangerous assignments, and refuses M's offer to drop his OO number, although he is made Head of Station J in Jamaica while he looks into Strangways's disappearance.

Bond's trusty Beretta, which he has used for fifteen years, is replaced by a Walther PPK on the advice of the Armorer, Major Boothroyd. He also carries a Smith & Wesson Centennial Airweight (which he later sarcastically informs M is ineffective against a flame-thrower). He still sleeps with his right hand holding the butt of his gun.

He bonds once more with the Jamaican, Quarrel, with whom he worked in *Live and Let Die* five years earlier, and who trains him again. He is violently sick after managing to kill a deadly centipede, which had been placed on his bed. He is highly protective of Honeychile Rider, the orphan girl he meets on Crab Key, but is still concerned that she makes an extra target for his enemies. He doesn't worry about singing in front of her—he knows the Jamaican calypso "Marion"—and fantasizes about sorting out her life. It's a long time since he's had to pay for sex—or, at least, pay for an "untrained" call girl. He doesn't sleep with Honey while they're on Crab Key, but promises to do so later, which she describes as "slave-time." He lies to her that they'll be safe, but sneers at himself for the lie, particularly as he feels guilty over Quarrel's death.

His capacity to deal with pain is put to the greatest test yet: as he goes through an obstacle course created by Dr. No, he is electrocuted, burned, and attacked by a giant squid, but his pulse remains slow and regular at the end. However, once the battle is over, he collapses "like a dead man" and relies on Honey to sail them back.

# GOLDFINGER

Bond's next assignment was against Auric Goldfinger in the 1959 novel named after the villain: a chance meeting in Miami pits the two men as enemies, and eventually Bond discovers that Goldfinger plans to rob Fort Knox of its gold. His only potential allies in Goldfinger's camp are Tilly Masterton and lesbian cat-burglar Pussy Galore.

The book opens with Bond thinking about life and death, and having some second thoughts about his profession, although he forces himself out of his reverie for a time (the feelings return when he is on night duty). He keeps his Walther PPK concealed within a book titled *The Bible Designed to be Read as Literature*, and he is planning to write a self-defense manual titled *Stay Alive!* He isn't aware of karate. His salary for being an 00 agent equates to $4,200 per annum; he has been in the section for six years. The mission against Goldfinger takes him to familiar territory, prompting memories of previous adventures, and when he believes the end is near, he trusts that 008 will be sent to replace him, with a license to kill the villain. Rather than use his own car, he drives an Aston Martin DB III with suitable modifications from the Service pool, including a compartment under the driver's seat in which to put his long-barreled Colt .45.

As a teenager, twenty years earlier, Bond played two rounds of golf every day of the week at the Royal St Marks golf course in Sandwich, Kent, where he was trained by Alfred Blacking. He is now a 9 handicap, and often plays at Huntercombe. He hates drinking tea. When contemplating a forced layover in Miami, he considers getting drunk for the first time in years, and being carried to bed by "whatever tart he had picked up." He ends up bedding Goldfinger's assistant, Jill Masterton, giving her the $10,000 fee that he receives for exposing Goldfinger as a cheat, and unsurprisingly he feels guilty when he learns she has been murdered. He has the same pangs of guilt when her sister, Tilly, is killed by Goldfinger's bowler-hatted henchman Oddjob later in the book. When in doubt about where to stay in a strange town, he chooses station hotels. The Loire valley is one of his favorite places in the world.

*The Pan UK release of Goldfinger in 1961 featured what looked like Ian Fleming himself in the background.*

For pleasure-reading, he chooses a book on golf and the latest Raymond Chandler novel.

Although attracted to her when she speeds past him in her car, he puts thoughts of Tilly Masterton aside until he realizes that she's also pursuing Goldfinger (at this point he doesn't know her name). He feels challenged by Pussy Galore's lesbianism, and registers that Tilly has sapphic leanings. He believes that they are a "herd of unhappy sexual misfits"—people who are neither gay nor straight—and feels sorry for them, but he has no time for them. Pussy changes sides (and sexual orientation), explaining that this is because she "never met a man before." Bond is bigoted against Koreans, regarding them as below apes in the mammalian hierarchy, and spends a lot of his time around Oddjob taunting him.

He is prepared to try to commit suicide by holding his own breath rather than succumb to Goldfinger's interrogation, but Goldfinger stops before he can see if he succeeds. He goes berserk, for the first time in his life, when he's fighting for his life with Goldfinger in their final confrontation.

## FOR YOUR EYES ONLY

In 1960, Bond returned in a collection of five short stories, *For Your Eyes Only*, some of which were based on plots Fleming had devised for a proposed Bond TV series.

Bond investigates the murder of a NATO dispatch rider in "From a View to a Kill." We learn that he lost his virginity in Paris aged sixteen at "Sank Roo Doe Noo," and when he is in the French capital, he always drinks Americanos, made with Perrier water, and smokes Laurens jaune cigarettes. He has not had a happy day in Paris since 1945, and plans on spending the evening with a high-class call girl to take his mind off a failed mission to extract a Hungarian over the Austrian border. He's ridden motorcycles some time previously. He makes the mistake of threatening Soviet agents with his gun still on safety, but his life is saved by the intervention of fellow agent Mary Ann Russell.

"For Your Eyes Only" sees Bond undertake a personal mission for M, volunteering to kill the murderers of some of his boss's friends. Bond's slightly flippant sense of humor continues to develop, addressing the

bow-carrying Judy Havelock as "Robina Hood." He's still under forty, and has never suffered a personal loss (his orphan status hasn't been revealed at this stage). He spends a moment fantasizing about what he wants to do to Judy (it involves spanking) before getting on with the mission.

In "Quantum of Solace," Bond reacts compassionately to a story he is being told, and realizes that ordinary life can be as dramatic as his missions—giving him a perspective on his own job that does not put it in a good light. He maintains that he would marry an air hostess if he ever did tie the knot. He is in the Bahamas to help foil plans by supporters of Fidel Castro (with whom—ironically—he sympathizes).

Bond is on the trail of a drug-smuggling ring in "Risico," after he's been moved from his usual work to assist Scotland Yard's battle against narcotics. He's horrified when his ally, Enrico Colombo, kisses him on both cheeks.

In "The Hildebrand Rarity," a rare type of fish of the same name as the story title is used to kill wife-beater Milton Krest—but neither his abused wife nor Bond's creole friend Fidele admits to the crime. Bond doesn't want to get involved in a domestic dispute, but after Krest's death, he disposes of the evidence that he was murdered—although he doesn't own up to that.

# THE SPECTRE YEARS
## THUNDERBALL

A new phase starts with 1961's *Thunderball*, as Bond encounters super-criminal group SPECTRE (Special Executive for Counterintelligence, Terrorism, Revenge and Extortion) for the first time when they hijack nuclear bombs. Bond is sent to the Bahamas and discovers the location of the bombs, with the assistance of Domino Vitali, the girlfriend of SPECTRE Number Two, Emilio Largo.

Bond is not in a good state at the start of this book: in addition to the many scars on his body, he's regularly hungover, and gambling stupidly. His medical report indicates that, against advice, he's smoking sixty cigarettes and drinking half a bottle of spirits a day, has slightly raised blood pressure, and suffers from headaches and fibrosis. As a result, M sends him to health-clinic, Shrublands, in Sussex, and his work is taken over by 009. His libido is re-energized while there, shortly before he is nearly killed on the traction table. Once recovered from that, the treatments mean his blood pressure is more normal, the fibrosis goes, and his weight reduces by ten pounds. He becomes a convert to the cause, eating healthily, switching cigarettes to low-tar Duke of Durhams with filters (and only ten of them a day), and giving up alcohol. He reverts to normal after witnessing a bomb blast and nearly being shot, so, when in Nassau, his gourmand tendencies reassert themselves. Domino Vitali thinks he's in his mid-thirties, and has "dark, rather cruel good looks."

Bond is intolerant of the younger generation and only thinks of a woman as a "tart" if she actually is a professional prostitute. He's not keen on women drivers, particularly if there are lots of them as passengers as well. He fantasizes about Domino, but knows that any encounter must come after he's finished the job—although he doesn't object when seducing her becomes part of his work, claiming that it's the first time he's eaten a woman (sic). He tries to close his mind to the almost-certain prospect of her death if she helps him.

He had to jump from the Arlberg Express around the time of the Hungarian uprising in 1956, and

*Richard Hawkey's innovative design for the 1963 Pan UK edition of* Thunderball *included two bullet holes die-cut into the cover.*

has only been on a submarine once before, while in the RNVR Special Branch (describing himself as a "chocolate sailor"—someone who sits behind a desk rather than going to sea).

## THE SPY WHO LOVED ME

The following year's Bond novel was a real departure—*The Spy Who Loved Me* is credited to "Ian Fleming with Vivienne Michel," and is a story told in the first person

by a Canadian girl who ends up needing Bond to save her from two gangsters who have come to burn down the motel she's supposed to be looking after. 007 doesn't appear until nearly two-thirds in to the story, and disposes of the two hoodlums on his way through.

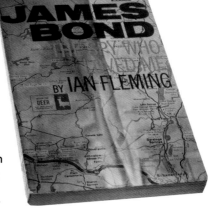

We see Bond (whom she always refers to as either James Bond or James) through Vivienne's eyes: good-looking "in a dark, rather cruel way," with a scar she claims is on his left cheek (it's on his right elsewhere). He's been on a mission to protect a defector in Toronto, and he's tired of seeing the aftermath of a gun battle. He's still taking Benzedrine to keep himself awake. He instantly involves himself in Vivienne's problems, taking down the two men, but he doesn't want her hanging on to his gun arm—literally, in this instance.

*The 1963 Pan UK cover showed the area of the Adirondack Mountains in which* The Spy Who Loved Me *is set.*

He claims that he's never been able to shoot someone down in cold blood. He makes love to her once the gangsters are dead, and he's the best lover she's ever had (even if she has some unusual opinions on what women like from a lover).

## ON HER MAJESTY'S SECRET SERVICE

*The Spy Who Loved Me* wasn't well-received, and Fleming returned to a more standard framework for *On Her Majesty's Secret Service* (*OHMSS*), published in 1963. The romantic element of *The Spy Who Loved Me* still appeared, though: *OHMSS* charts Bond falling in love with Contessa Teresa di Vicenzo (Tracy) and their marriage—and her death at the hands of Ernst Stavro Blofeld, head of SPECTRE, and his mistress Irma Bunt, whose plan to wage germ warfare from their base in the Alps has just been thwarted by 007.

Bond is still feeling disenchanted with his job, and is mentally writing his resignation letter; ever since *Thunderball*, he has been on Blofeld's trail rather than an active part of the OO section. However, when he is told that Blofeld is in Switzerland, he regains his urgency. All members of the Service now carry Syncraphones (an early pager), and when his beeps, he calls his new secretary, Mary Goodnight. He has an uncanny knowledge of how SPECTRE operates, despite never having been at one of their meetings. He has to disavow knowledge of a fellow agent when he threatens to blow Bond's cover in Blofeld's base at Piz Gloria, but Bond maintains his composure. He takes two weeks' leave to enable him to work with the Unione Corse to bring down Blofeld.

He is attracted to Tracy as soon as she drives past him at speed, and he pays her debts at the casino later that evening. After they spend the night together, he is worried that she's going to commit suicide, and he is thanked for his kindness in trying to save Tracy by her father, Marc-Ange Draco, the leader of the Unione Corse. Bond is happy to see Tracy again, once she has had suitable psychiatric treatment, and as a result he doesn't pursue Mary Goodnight further, instead sending Tracy encouraging letters mailed in America. (However, his affection for her doesn't prevent him from seducing Ruby, one of Blofeld's unwitting pawns at Piz Gloria, in the line of duty.) After Tracy helps him to escape from Blofeld's thugs, he realizes that he loves her, and asks her to marry him (which causes him to have a nightmare of respectability). He turns down the dowry Draco offers.

Bond spent childhood summers at the beach with his parents, and has skied in the Alps many times before, although he hasn't skied for some time: the bindings and skis themselves are different from his day. He was taught to ski at the Hannes Schneider School at St. Anton in the Arlberg by Herr Fuchs, and uses every ounce of his knowledge to evade Blofeld's men, exhausting himself in the process. He also knows how to ride a skeleton-bobsleigh. He has spent some time in Marseilles, as well as "the dirtiest bar in Singapore."

He has had his Bentley for three years, and every year he makes a pilgrimage to Vesper Lynd's grave at Royale-les-Eaux. His father was a Scot, from the Highlands, near Glencoe, and his mother was Swiss; his family coat of arms is "*argent on a chevron sable three bezants"*—which means it has three golden balls—and the motto is "The World is not Enough." He now reads the *Daily Express* (*The Times* is an "extra badge of Top Peopleship") as well as Rex Stout's Nero Wolfe mysteries, and wears a Rolex watch.

# YOU ONLY LIVE TWICE

The final novel in the Blofeld trilogy, *You Only Live Twice* was the last to be published in Fleming's lifetime, and sees a broken Bond sent out to Japan, where, to his surprise, he encounters Blofeld one last time. The former SPECTRE head is hiding out on an island with a Garden of Death; Bond is sent to infiltrate it by the Japanese Secret Service and manages to kill Blofeld and Irma Bunt, but in the process falls from a balloon and suffers amnesia. His superiors believe he has been killed.

Bond took a month's leave after Tracy's death, part of which he spent in Jamaica. He then bungled two missions in the period before the book starts. He's drinking too much (counting the hours to his next drink), and gambling very heavily, to the extent that M starts to believe he may be a security risk. Bond's aware of his situation, but hasn't been able to shake himself free of the malaise. M, however, takes the advice of Sir James Molony and gives him an "impossible" assignment and promotion to the diplomatic section, code number 7777. In the past, Bond has deliberately steered clear of too much knowledge about the Service's cryptography secrets in case he is captured and interrogated. Mary Goodnight has been with him for three years at the time of his "death."

M writes Bond's obituary, which fills in some of the gaps in his personal life, but which also contradicts earlier details supplied by Fleming. He was born in 1924 (the Year of the Rat in Chinese astrology), making him still under forty; his parents were Andrew Bond and Monique Delacroix. They were killed in a climbing accident in the Aiguilles Rouges when Bond was 11, and he passed into the guardianship of his aunt Charmian in Pett Bottom, Kent. He was at Eton for two halves before some alleged trouble with one of the boys' maids, and he transferred to Fettes in Scotland. He was a lightweight boxer and judo expert, and in 1941, claiming to be 19 rather than 17, joined up, entering the Special Branch of the RNVR, and rising to Commander at the end of the war. He was awarded the CMG in 1954, and got married in 1962. A series of books was written about him by a former colleague.

Bond starts to regain some self-respect and interest through his interaction with Japanese Secret Service chief Tiger Tanaka, and is intrigued by the prospect of encountering Dr. Shatterhand, keeper of poisonous plants, even before he realizes that it's Blofeld—although he deliberately chooses to keep the knowledge of Blofeld's identity from Tanaka, so he can gain revenge. His sense of humor is now quite biting and his patriotism comes to the fore, defending Britain to Tanaka, but he agrees to adopt a Japanese disguise for the mission. He believes suicide is cowardly. He is trained in ninja ways, which he uses to kill Blofeld, and learns to be a fisherman thanks to Ama-diver Kissy Suzuki, who rescues him and looks after him when he develops amnesia after his fall from the balloon. His condition extends to how to make love, until Kissy buys a "pillow book," and she soon becomes pregnant. She doesn't tell him he's going to be a father before he leaves for Vladivostok.

## THE MAN WITH THE GOLDEN GUN

Ian Fleming's final Bond novel, *The Man with the Golden Gun*, was published posthumously, and feels like an attempt to get the agent back on track. After recovering from the brainwashing he receives from the KGB, Bond is sent back to Jamaica, where he infiltrates the retinue of hitman Francisco "Pistols" Scaramanga, eventually killing the assassin.

Bond has been missing for a year, during which time he went from Japan to Vladivostok, from there to Moscow, and a military airfield at Vtoraya Rechka, and finally he spent some time in the hands of "Colonel Boris" of the KGB at an institute on the Nevsky Prospekt in Leningrad, where he was brainwashed into trying to kill M. The KGB believe Bond lives the high life, so he stays at the Ritz. He is no longer smoking his special Morlands. After the attack on M fails, he is sent to The Park to be looked after by Sir James Molony, and then he is used as a tool against Scaramanga. His old secretary, Mary Goodnight, is stationed in Jamaica; when Bond fantasizes about her at a time that he

*Roger Moore protects Maud Adams and Britt Ekland in this 1974 tie-in edition of* The Man with the Golden Gun *for Pan UK.*

should be concentrating on the assignment, he takes a cold shower. His obituary was reprinted by American newspapers.

Once cured by electric-shock treatment, he adopts his old patterns, reading the *Daily Gleaner* in Jamaica, and enjoying spending time there. He's smoking about twenty-five cigarettes a day, and drinking, but not as heavily as before. His mocking sense of humor also returns, and his enjoyment of a mission: even when things are at their most tense, he doesn't display any real stress. He still dislikes cold murder, and doesn't take out Scaramanga when he has the chance because he would also need to kill his chauffeur—although he knows he's being a "bloody fool." He gets careless when he drinks more than he should and shows off his prowess with a gun, which blows his cover with Scaramanga. At the end of the mission, he's shot by Scaramanga with a bullet dipped in snake venom, and he takes a week to regain consciousness.

He was in Berlin in 1945, and is a member of the Twin Snakes Club, the fraternity of ex-Secret Service men who meet at Blades once a year. The Prime Minister proposes to recommend Bond for a knighthood, so he's a KCMG, which M supports. He refuses it, partly because he doesn't want to pay more at hotels and restaurants, but mainly because he is a Scottish peasant and will always feel at home being a Scottish peasant.

## *OCTOPUSSY*

Fleming wrote four further short stories featuring 007, which are now collected as *Octopussy*. In the title story, set around 1961, he is sent to question Major Dexter Smythe about the theft of Nazi gold at the end of the war, during which the major killed ski instructor Hannes Oberhauser—who taught Bond pre-war, and was "something of a father" to Bond "when I happened to need one." He allows Smythe the opportunity to commit suicide rather than be tried.

"The Living Daylights" is what Bond scares out of a KGB assassin he has been sent to kill—to enable an agent to cross from East to West Berlin safely at what will become Checkpoint Charlie—but instead chooses to spare. He's had his Bentley Continental adapted to make it a real two-seater with plenty of luggage space. He takes a couple of Tuinal sleeping pills to ensure that he rests before the assignment.

*Ian Fleming pictured in 1963 outside the Royal Courts of Justice in London during the court case over the genesis of Thunderball.*

He's slightly distracted by a pretty girl with a cello—who is actually the assassin—which explains why he chooses to frighten her off rather than kill her. When the local liaison complains, he says that with any luck it'll cost him his job.

"The Property of a Lady" is a Fabergé "terrestrial globe" that is being auctioned to pay off a Soviet mole in the Secret Service, and which Bond sees as an opportunity to flush out the KGB's Resident Director in London. He has never been to an auction before. His skin crawls when he has to spend time with the mole, Maria Freudenstein.

"007 in New York" is a very short story, originally contained within Fleming's non-fiction book *Thrilling Cities*. Bond is sent to America to persuade a former Service secretary to dump her boyfriend, whom she doesn't realize is a KGB agent, before the CIA and FBI learn who she is. Bond once had a small apartment in New York, and regrets the way the city has changed. He still knows the best places to eat and drink (and the chefs are willing to cook scrambled eggs to his recipe—provided in the book) and is meeting a long-term lover, Solange, while there. His knowledge of the town isn't encyclopedic—there is no reptile house at the Central Park Zoo, which is where he sets his rendezvous with the girl.

# THE CARS

James Bond has always loved his cars. According to Ian Fleming, he purchased his first vehicle in 1933—when he was barely a teenager (the explanation as to how an orphaned schoolboy could afford one at such a tender age is given in Charlie Higson's Young Bond novel *Double or Die*)—and this love of automobiles has been displayed in every form of media in which his adventures have appeared.

The car most associated with 007 is the Aston Martin DB5. Produced between 1963 and 1966, only 1,059 were made, and they were capable of accelerating from 0 to 60 mph in 7.1 seconds and attaining a top speed of 148 mph. Bond's original model, license plate BMT 216A, first appeared in *Goldfinger*, then made a further bow in *Thunderball*. This was the car that was fully equipped by Q with bulletproof glass at the front, sides and rear; revolving license plates; smoke screen; oil screen; rear bulletproof screen; and left and right front-wing machine guns. And, of course, there's the *pièce de résistance*: the passenger ejector seat, operated from within the gearstick. Between the films, rear water cannons had also been fitted. The exact same car met its end in *Skyfall*—its front-wing machine guns still lethally effective to the last.

Pierce Brosnan's 007 drove a different DB5 (license BMT 214A) in his first two movies, *Golden-Eye* and *Tomorrow Never Dies*, which isn't as well modified—although, conveniently, there's a chilled compartment in which to place champagne, and it has a communications uplink to use in conjunction with his zoom camera. Daniel Craig's Bond acquired a DB5 in *Casino Royale*, winning it in a poker game from Alex Dimitrios.

The DB5 wasn't Bond's first Aston Martin. In the *Goldfinger* novel, he was given a "DB III" (which

doesn't really exist; Fleming presumably meant the DB Mark III), which was retrofitted with switches to alter the shape and color of the front and rear lights, reinforced steel fenders, a Colt .45 in a hidden compartment beneath the driver's seat, radio tracking equipment, and plenty of concealed space. This was the only time in the original books

*Honor Blackman (Pussy Galore from 1964's Goldfinger) and Christopher Lee (Scaramanga in The Man with the Golden Gun a decade later) at a 2002 exhibition of the Bond cars.*

that Bond drives a gadget-laden car, and it was the inspiration for the movie version, and its successors.

Aston Martins appear in twelve Bond films so far—as producer Michael G. Wilson explained when the DB5's presence in *Skyfall* was revealed, "We've used different cars from time to time, but we always do come back to Aston Martin." A DBS is driven by 007 in *OHMSS*, but this one clearly hasn't been specially equipped by Q—if it had been fitted with bulletproof glass like its predecessors, Bond wouldn't have been widowed.

The Aston Martin V8 that Bond "takes for a spin" in *The Living Daylights* is rather better equipped with a few "optional extras." When pursued by the Bratislavan police, Bond opens a compartment featuring controls for port and star-

*James Bond's Aston Martin as seen in Pierce Brosnan's debut film, GoldenEye, in 1995.*

board lasers; missiles; a rocket motor; and an outrigger complete with spikes for the tires. All

of these are used in the subsequent chase, as well as the rear bulletproof glass, but after the V8 doesn't survive the impact with a tree, Bond sets the automatic destruct.

The V12 Vanquish acquired the nickname the "Vanish" because of its light-refracting capabilities—an upgrade to the car that was a step too far for many fans. Seen in *Die Another Day*, it possessed "Adaptive Camouflage"—tiny cameras on all sides of the vehicle which projected an image

onto special material on the other side to make it seem invisible—as well as the "usual refinements": ejector seat, traction spikes, torpedoes, front-wing machine guns, laser, grenades, mortars, and target-seeking shotguns. When Bond faces henchman Zao in his similarly well-equipped Jaguar XKR, he needs all of these to survive.

In addition to winning a classic DB5 in *Casino Royale*, 007 is issued with a company car—the latest from Aston Martin, the DBS V12. It doesn't survive its sevenfold roll through the Montenegrin countryside (in reality, a record-breaking stunt from Gary Powell's team, who used a modified DB9 as the DBS wasn't ready in time), and it doesn't have the gizmos that audiences might have expected. Instead, there's a defibrillator, a combi-pen containing antidotes to poisons, and a compartment for Bond's Walther PPK. A new DBS featured at the start of *Quantum of Solace*. Like the DBS in *OHMSS*, this hasn't apparently received any modifications: the windows shatter easily, and to fend off the attention of Quantum's bodyguards, Bond has to resort to his own Heckler & Koch machine pistol.

In *SPECTRE*, Bond drives the new Aston Martin DB10, which features in a car chase through Rome. In fact, on this occasion the DB10 really is a Bond car—this is a model that was developed specifically for the film and built in-house by the brand's design and engineering teams; only ten are being made.

Other car manufacturers have made multiple appearances in the Bond franchise, too. In the early books, and the movie of *From Russia with Love*, Bond drives a Bentley (a Mark IV in the film); in the novels, it's a 1930 4½-litre version with an Amherst Villiers supercharger, which he drove "hard and well and with an almost sensual pleasure." That's destroyed when 007 is chasing after Hugo Drax in *Moonraker*, although Bond replaces it with a 1953 Mark VI at the end of that novel. By the time of *Thunderball*, that too has been replaced, with a Mark II Continental, which Bond spends considerable time and money upgrading with a new engine and supercharger. He's still driving that in the mid-1960s in Sebastian Faulks's *Devil May Care* and Robert Markham's *Colonel Sun*. Many years later, in John Gardner's *Role of Honor*, Bond buys a brand new Bentley Mulsanne Turbo to fulfill an unusual request in his uncle's will. This is kitted out with a phone and a weapons compartment, but no other gadgets, since Bentley asked Gardner not to otherwise customize it. Bond still maintains this car as late as Raymond Benson's *High Time to Kill*, published in 1999. The rebooted Bond seen in Jeffery Deaver's *Carte Blanche* drives a Bentley Continental GT, the latest in a number he has owned.

Roger Moore's Bond drives two cars that have stuck in the memories of 007 fans: the AMC Hornet, which spirals over the river in *The Man with the Golden Gun*, and the convertible submarine Lotus Esprit, which features in *The Spy Who Loved Me*. The Hornet—which 007 blithely drives out of a showroom with Sheriff J.W. Pepper (Clifton James) aboard—was actually used for the stunt (contrary to the impression given by the whistle on the soundtrack), which required hours of calculations on the rudimentary computers of 1973. That film also features Scaramanga's flying AMC Hornet, which wasn't a real car!

The Lotus Esprit is a proper MI6 "company car," filled with gadgetry courtesy of Q—although it was clearly not as secret as Major Boothroyd might have hoped, since the KGB's Major Amasova knew how to operate its controls! It can convert from a car (equipped with a cement sprayer) into a submarine, complete with surface-to-air missiles, smoke screens, and limpet mines. Entrepreneur and inventor Elon Musk of Tesla Motors bought the original model for nearly a million pounds at auction in September 2013. "What I'm going to do is upgrade it with a Tesla electric powertrain and try to make it transform for real," he announced. A Lotus Esprit Turbo made a brief appearance in *For Your Eyes Only*, but self-destructed when touched by one of Gonzales's henchmen; it was "reconstituted" (according to Q) in red for a scene later in the film. The original automobile's destruction led to one of the more unusual car chases, with 007 not feeling at all at home behind the wheel of a Citroën 2CV.

Pierce Brosnan's Bond was most associated with BMW cars: the Z3 roadster was featured briefly in *GoldenEye*, with Q explaining that it had all-points radar, self-destruct system, and "all the usual refinements," including Stinger missiles behind the headlights.

*The famous Lotus Esprit from* The Spy Who Loved Me *in underwater mode.*

However, it never got a chance to display its potential—in reality, because the deal between EON and BMW came too late in production. However, the next BMW more than made up for that: the 750iL (whose license plate BMT 2144 is very close to that of Brosnan's Aston Martin) seen in *Tomorrow Never Dies* could be operated by remote control from Bond's cell phone, and was stocked with machine guns, rockets, GPS tracking, smoke canisters, tire-shredding tacks, reinflatable tires, and a wire cutter underneath the hood badge. The Z8 that Bond drove in *The World Is Not Enough* also didn't get much chance to display its abilities beyond a surface-to-air missile before it was bisected by a buzz saw.

In the books, John Gardner decided that Bond would choose a Saab 900 Turbo, which 007 nicknamed the "Silver Beast" and had equipped with extra gadgets recommended by the (real-life company) Communication Control Systems Ltd.

When he took over, Raymond Benson upgraded Bond to a Jaguar XK8, which Q Branch suitably modified with adaptable camouflage paint, heat-seeking rockets, cruise missiles, a holographic projector, and a flying scout, which could be sent out from the car to drop mines on the enemy. Charlie Higson's *Young Bond* novels indicated that James's first car was a Bamford & Martin 1.5 Litre Side Valve Short Chassis Tourer, which he inherited from his uncle. It was destroyed in *Double or Die*, leading to his purchase of the Bentley. Most recently, William Boyd thought Bond would pick the new Jensen FF in 1969, while his Bentley was off the road in *Solo*.

Of course, these are only the cars that Bond *chooses* to drive—as we have seen on countless occasions, he can master any vehicle. However, as Q points out in *GoldenEye*, "Need I remind you, 007, that you have a licence to kill, not break the traffic laws!"

# CHAPTER 003

# BOND IN OTHER MEDIA

JAMES BOND'S ADVENTURES HAVE APPEARED IN MANY DIFFERENT MEDIA, BUT ONE OF THE LONGEST-RUNNING VERSIONS HAS ESCAPED MANY FANS' ATTENTION: THE COMIC STRIP. IAN FLEMING WASN'T PARTICULARLY KEEN ON SEEING A COMIC-STRIP ADAPTATION OF HIS JAMES BOND STORIES. AFTER THE BRUISING EXPERIENCE OF *CASINO ROYALE*'S JOURNEY TO TELEVISION (SEE CHAPTER 13), HE HAD GRAVE RESERVATIONS ABOUT ANYTHING THAT MIGHT JEOPARDIZE HIS SUCCESS.

However, he eventually agreed that Lord Beaverbrook's *Daily Express* newspaper could run versions of the stories, starting in 1958, and illustrated by John McLusky from scripts mainly by Henry Gammidge (although Anthony Hern penned *Casino Royale*, and *Modesty Blaise* creator Peter O'Donnell adapted *Dr. No*).

Fleming provided an illustration of how he believed Bond should appear, but McLusky updated what he saw as a pre-World War II look, providing the template for the strip version of 007 that would be published worldwide until 1984. The comic strips were pretty faithful adaptations of the novels and three of the short stories from *For Your Eyes Only*, although some of the sadism and torture occurred "off-panel."

There was a slight hiccup during the telling of *Thunderball*. After a disagreement with Fleming over the rights to the short story "The Living Daylights," Beaverbrook cancelled the strip—a single wrap-up was hastily commissioned—and it was two years before the story picked up with *OHMSS*, which was mid-run when Fleming died. The newspaper continued with *You Only Live Twice* before Gammidge left.

However, for nearly twenty years afterward, from 1966 to 1984, original stories featuring 007 appeared in British newspaper strips, which were syndicated around the world. All thirty-three of the scripts for these new tales were penned by one man, J.D. (Jim) Lawrence, making him by far the most prolific, and longest-running, writer of Bond stories.

Lawrence took over writing duties on the strip in 1965, with his first story, a version of *The Man with the Golden Gun*, arriving in January 1966. He was responsible for adapting Fleming's stories "The Living Daylights," "Octopussy," "The Hildebrand Rarity," and *The Spy Who Loved Me*, but rather than faithfully translating the tales into the new medium, he added extra subplots—and in the case of *The Spy Who Loved Me*, a complete new adventure, reintroducing SPECTRE to the strip, which preceded Bond's arrival at the motel.

Although some Fleming stories had not been adapted, Lawrence was given permission by Glidrose to create new tales, at a time when they were also commissioning Kingsley Amis to continue the saga under the pen name Robert Markham. (Lawrence also adapted *Colonel Sun* for the strip, although he changed the villains from Red China to SPECTRE to fit with his own continuity.) The new stories originally appeared in the *Daily Express*, before the strip transferred first to the *Sunday Express*, and eventually to the *Daily Star* (all part of the same newspaper group). The *Daily Star* dropped the strip mid-story in July 1983, although foreign syndication continued for three more tales, eventually concluding in 1984.

Lawrence was an American writer, who worked predominantly with Russian artist Yaroslav Horak on the strip, and the two would collaborate on the plots. For Lawrence, a Bond story had to have "action going, you've got to have T and A . . . you have to have colorful villains. And the colorful villain often has to be involved with some kind of super-scientific weapon." In an interview he gave five years after finishing work on Bond, Lawrence pointed out that there were sides to the agent with which he was less enamored. "Things I didn't approve of I suppose I soft-pedaled, and did it my way insofar as it was in keeping with the character," he explained.

The strip Bond is far more ruthless than the screen incarnation—particularly once Roger Moore started to play the character with a lighter touch—and is willing to do whatever it takes to achieve his aims. Although there are times that he is unwilling to blackmail innocents—he queries M about the idea pointedly in the story "The Phoenix Project," before knuckling under when his superior tells him to "spare me your sentimental drivel"—he usually is merciless. He enjoys the company of many different ladies throughout the strip, but he doesn't try to seduce every woman he meets. In the wonderfully titled "Die With My Boots On," he doesn't become involved with either of the female leads, and he has a strong working relationship with a fellow OO agent, Suzi Kew, whose maturation as an agent we follow across the years (although they do eventually become lovers). He's no feminist: his epitaph on the villainess Gretta in "Trouble Spot" is, "Can't blame a woman for wanting to survive. She'd no man to look after her."

He has a sadistic streak to him, even pausing while suffering from a potentially lethal gas infection to twist a girl's arm behind her back and let her know he's "rather enjoying this." He's not politically correct at all: when he discovers that there's gold in a casket that should contain a Chinese body, he notes, "At least something in the coffin is yellow."

He initially has an apartment in Earls Court, London, under his current regular alias of Mark Hazard, but he moves to a penthouse apartment later in the run. He uses a Beretta once more—but speaks in a rather less refined way than Bond usually does (classic lines from "The Golden Ghost" include, "Blimey! I feel downright naked without that friendly little Beretta under my arm!" which wouldn't be out of place in *Austin Powers*, and, "Just caution luv . . . I never did dig that Light Brigade jive!" in "The Girl Machine"). Contrary to what you might expect from his speech patterns, he's a devotee of the writer Robert Louis Stevenson, although this would fit with Lawrence's admission that, for him, the character of Bond was defined by Sean

*The surreal cover painted by Mike Grell for issue 3 of his 1989 synthesis of book and movie Bond,* Permission to Die.

Connery's performance, even if Horak and John McLusky, in his second spell on the comic, kept to the visual portrayal of Bond created for the strip in 1958.

Lawrence did add a quite unusual note to Bond's résumé: in "The Harpies," he turns down a knighthood for the second time (the first is in *The Man with the Golden Gun*) before (apparently) accepting one in "The Paradise Plot." (The English text is ambiguous; the overseas version less so, referring to him as "Sir James.")

Jim Lawrence wasn't the only comic-strip writer to tackle Bond's adventures; unfortunately, most of the others that did stuck to a portrayal of the agent that was anodyne and didn't really add anything to the mythos. Although fresh graphic versions of Fleming's original stories were meant to be published by Dynamite Entertainment in 2015, no further details have yet been released.

Mike Grell's *Permission to Die*, however, published in 1989, successfully amalgamated the then current Bond of the books (as created by John Gardner) with a Timothy Dalton-esque 007. His Bond smokes triple-ringed cigarettes, uses an ASP 9mm, and still retains May as his housekeeper, but 007's Service colleagues (M and Q) are definitely the film variants. With some acerbic one-liners, and a plot that lived up to Jim Lawrence's requirements for a Bond story, this can be seen as a neat capping of the comic-strip saga.

## THE AUDIO BOND

Only one radio production of a Bond script occurred during Ian Fleming's lifetime: a South African version of *Moonraker*, starring future British TV game-show host Bob Holness as Bond, was broadcast in 1956, although sadly no recording of this survives. Bond returned to the airwaves thirty-four years later in a one-off version of *You Only Live Twice*, starring Michael Jayston—who had played novelist Adam Hall's antithesis of James Bond, Quiller, for a BBC TV series in 1975. This is regularly repeated on the BBC's digital station, Radio 4 Extra, and captures the languor of the book admirably.

Four further stories have appeared in recent years, each starring Toby Stephens— the villainous Gustav Graves from *Die Another Day*—as Bond. EON granted production company Jarvis & Ayres special permission for *Dr. No* to be adapted by Hugh Whitemore to mark the centenary of Fleming's birth in 2008, with *Poirot*'s David Suchet donning the villain's steel pincers. John Standing played M, with future *Doctor Who*

Peter Capaldi as the armorer, Major Boothroyd, and Lisa Dillon as Honey-chile Rider. According to producer and director Martin Jarvis (who also voiced the narrator in the play), EON were so impressed that they asked the company to continue, and in 2010 came Archie Scottney's version of *Goldfinger*, with *X-Men* and *Lord of the Rings* star Ian McKellen as Bond's opponent, and Stephens's *Die Another Day* co-star Rosamund Pike as Pussy Galore. The team selected from earlier in the Bond canon for the third play, Scottney's adaptation of *From Russia, with Love*, which aired in 2012. Nathaniel Parker played Red Grant, with Mark Gatiss as master planner Kronsteen and Eileen Atkins as Rosa Klebb. The story was streamlined considerably, removing the Krilencu subplot from the tale.

Jarvis & Ayres moved forward to the second of the Blofeld tales for the most recent adaptation (*Thunderball*'s undersea setting would not make it ideal for radio!). *OHMSS* was recorded in May 2013, with *Absolutely Fabulous* star (and original *OHMSS* Bond Girl) Joanna Lumley as Tracy opposite Stephens's Bond.

Stephens's interpretation of Bond was described by the *Guardian* as "rather more boyish than his suave screen incarnations . . . and closer to Ian Fleming's style." Listened to in conjunction with the comic-strip versions, these plays produce something much closer to Fleming's intentions than some of the screenplays!

# THE GADGETS

For many people, the tour around Q's workshop is one of the highlights of the James Bond film series. In many of the movies between *Goldfinger* and *Die Another Day*, Bond arrives as Q is testing some weird gadget, and is shown all the items that he might (and, of course, usually will) need on his next mission. The scenes were often shot at the end of production to ensure that they foreshadowed events correctly. Desmond Llewelyn, then John Cleese, were our guides to this house of mechanical wonders. Quite a few of the gadgets were the sort of items you'd expect a secret agent to need—homing beacons, tracking devices, bug detectors—but there were many exceptional items provided by Q Branch, some of which did indeed exist in the real world, but that weren't commonplace at the time.

In *From Russia with Love*, Bond was given a briefcase containing a rifle and ammunition, gold sovereigns, a throwing knife, and tear-gas pellets which activated when the case was incorrectly opened. In addition to the many improvements to his car in *Goldfinger*, Bond was given another briefcase (which exploded), and at the start of the film he wears a wetsuit with a duck on top. Things started to get more extraordinary in *Thunderball*, in which Bond used a jet pack, as well as a super-powered scuba tank and a "rebreather" to allow him to stay mobile underwater for longer. By *You Only Live Twice*, he was even acquiring items from the Japanese Secret Service, such as a poison-dart firing cigarette.

"This time I've got the gadgets, Q," George Lazenby's Bond pointed out to Q on his wedding day, and *OHMSS* steps back from the over-reliance on Q's equipment, with a safe-cracking gizmo the only item on display. Connery's return for *Diamonds Are Forever* saw him use fake fingerprints, while Q invented a gadget to create jackpots on fruit machines; the original 007's final foray, in *Never Say Never Again*, featured an exploding pen (which still needed work, according to 007, after it fired late).

Roger Moore's seven films took the gadgetry to extremes at times, although his tenure started off in *Live and Let Die* with a nice gag about Bond's magnetic Rolex wristwatch being great for removing Italian agents' dresses, but less useful when he needed it to draw a boat toward him. A radio transmitter disguised as a hairbrush was rather more helpful. *The Man with the Golden Gun*'s main "gadget" was the gun the villainous Scaramanga (Christopher Lee) created from his lighter, cigarette case, fountain pen, and cuff link, which overshadowed Q's best contribution, Bond's fake nipple! *The*

*The most famous Q of them all, Desmond Llewelyn, surrounded by some of the many Bond gadgets including the Goldeneye device (center), the robot spy camera from A View to a Kill (back left), and the grenade pen from Goldeneye (in Llewelyn's hand).*

chase—although Bond's watch was still a radio receiver/transmitter. The timepiece gained more capabilities for *Octopussy*, while 007's pen also contained acid and an earpiece at separate times. Bond infiltrated Octopussy's island inside a fake crocodile, and a fake horse trailer disguised his miniature Acrostar airplane. Moore's farewell performance, in *A View to a Kill*, saw Bond discovered in the shower with Stacey Sutton (Tanya Roberts) by Snooper, a small animal-shaped robot operated by Q, and the agent used a credit-card electronic lock-pick.

*Spy Who Loved Me*, however, marked the start of the gadgetry taking over: Bond's watch included a miniature teleprinter; his ski poles fired explosive charges; his backpack contained a parachute (emblazoned, not particularly inconspicuously, with the Union Jack); his case and lighter combined to form a microfilm reader; and a razor-sharp tea tray was being prepared in Q's lab.

Everything was pushed to the limit in *Moonraker*: Bond used a wrist-controlled dart gun (which he only wore at the times he somehow knew he'd need it!); his watch had explosives within it; the cigarette case now became a safe-cracking aide; but perhaps most ridiculously, his gondola could convert into a hovercraft, allowing the secret agent to drive around St. Mark's Square in Venice. When the CIA's Holly Goodhead (Lois Chiles) also got in on the act with her own poison pen and flamethrower, it became clear that the gadgets were taking on too much importance.

*For Your Eyes Only* was a return to basics—marked by the early destruction of Bond's Lotus and the use of a Citroën 2CV for the car

*The front-wing machine gun (above) and its control (right) contained within Bond's Aston Martin, as used to devastating effect in Goldfinger.*

*Interior (left) and exterior (above) of the one-man aircraft, the Acrostar, as seen in the pre-credits sequence of Octopussy in 1983.*

he'd used it once, in complete contradiction of his usual hectoring of 007 to look after the gadgets!

Pierce Brosnan's time in the 00 section also saw the use of gadgets steadily accelerate. In *GoldenEye*, Bond had a belt with a piton and wire, as well as an exploding pen. His watch now had a laser cutter, and his binoculars had a satellite uplink. (There were also multiple gadgets in preparation in the lab.) *Tomorrow Never Dies* featured a mobile phone with multiple extra uses, as well as the usual exploding wristwatch and cigarette lighter. Chinese agent Wai Ling had her own arsenal of gadgets.

*The World Is Not Enough* began with Bond using an exploding gun, operated by special glasses, before he needed the hook and wire contained in his watch, the lock-pick disguised as a credit card, or the ski jacket which became an escape pod. That was nothing compared with *Die Another Day*, which showcased many of the old gadgets as well

Timothy Dalton's 007 was much more down to earth, although for *The Living Daylights* he was equipped with a keychain that could emit stun gas, be used as a lock-pick, or explode as required, and he used clip-over binoculars on normal glass frames. *Licence to Kill* included more gadgetry: plastic explosives disguised as toothpaste; an exploding alarm clock; a signature camera gun; and a laser Polaroid camera. Q also used a radio disguised as a garden rake—which he discarded after

which Q responds: "Were you expecting an exploding pen? We don't really go in for that anymore."

But some things never change; Q's last line to Bond in *Skyfall* echoes those of his predecessors: "Please return the equipment in one piece." In the world of 007, that simply doesn't happen often!

as virtual-reality glasses, a special ring that could cut unbreakable glass, a well-equipped surfboard, a watch with explosives and laser-beam cutter, and another miniature air supply.

Although most cars don't come equipped with a portable defibrillator, there weren't any unusual gadgets provided for Bond in *Casino Royale*, or *Quantum of Solace*—indeed, Q didn't even appear. When the "new quartermaster" meets Bond in the National Gallery in London in *Skyfall* and only provides a gun and a radio, the agent's comment is telling. "Not exactly Christmas, is it?" he says, to

*ABOVE: 007's cell phone that doubled as a remote control device for his BMW in 1997's Tomorrow Never Dies.*
*RIGHT: Charles Fraser-Smith, an inventor of SOE during World War II, who is sometimes credited as the inspiration for Q.*

# CHAPTER 004

# THE OTHER LITERARY BONDS:

## FROM ROBERT MARKHAM TO ANTHONY HOROWITZ

### COLONEL SUN

Ian Fleming's death in 1964 did not mark the end of the literary Bond's adventures. Fleming left behind an unpublished novel—*The Man with the Golden Gun*—as well as a number of short stories not yet collected between hard covers, which were presented to the devotees by his literary heirs, Glidrose Productions. However, with the movie series going from strength to strength with Sean Connery as Bond, and the newspaper strip continuing to prove popular, particularly since author Jim Lawrence was expanding on Fleming's prose for his adaptations, there was obviously a hunger for new 007 tales. There was also a practical consideration regarding keeping control of the character under literary copyright law.

Glidrose therefore decided to commission a new 007 novel, turning first to author James Leasor and then, after he turned them down, to British writer Kingsley Amis, who had previously written *The James Bond Dossier*, an in-depth analysis of

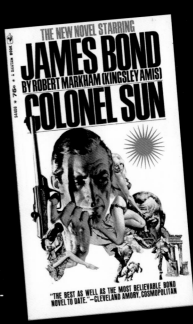

**OPPOSITE:** *Kingsley Amis, author of* The James Bond Dossier *and the first official continuation novel,* Colonel Sun, *under the penname Robert Markham.* **ABOVE:** *The 1969 Bantam edition of* Colonel Sun.

Fleming's character. Amis's story, *Colonel Sun*, was credited to Robert Markham, a pseudonym that Glidrose considered using as a "house name" for future Bond adventures, masking the identities of the different authors involved. In the end, however, no further stories were published using that name. Amis proposed an idea about an elderly Bond, which was turned down flat by Glidrose, and the trustees also refused to accept Geoffrey Jenkins's continuation novel *Per Fine Ounce*.

As the first person to pen a prose Bond story after Fleming, Amis was aware that he needed to keep the character consistent with the original, and *Colonel Sun*, set a year or so after the events of *The Man with the Golden Gun*, provides plenty of opportunity for the sex, sadism, and snobbery that went hand in hand with Bond's adventures. When M is kidnapped, Bond follows the trail to the Greek islands, where he teams up with KGB agent Ariadne Alexandrou to battle the Red Chinese agent Colonel Sun.

Amis didn't try to make Bond an expert on everything: when Bond is asked about boats and sailing, he admits he knows "a bit" because he "spent a lot of summer holidays years ago in a converted Brixham trawler" (a high-speed deep-sea fishing trawler). His daydreams during his developing years were apparently haunted by the character of the Black Stone, the villain in John Buchan's spy novel, *The Thirty-Nine Steps*. He does know about the finer sides of Greek cuisine, both food and drink—Amis admitted he enjoyed the research involved—and can speak some Greek, although Russian is beyond him. He smokes Macedonian Xanthi cigarettes when he's in Greece (he regards cigarette smoke as "life-giving" when he's recovering from being drugged). He's started to fall into a routine since his work for the Secret Service has become rather monotonous—he hasn't had a major mission in over a year—but once he sets out to seek revenge for the death of M's servants, the Hammonds, as well as his superior's kidnapping, the old instincts fall into place, and he can be almost excessively brutal at times.

There are times when Bond queries what he's doing—a common theme in the later Fleming stories—and he recognizes that, to an extent, he's a prisoner of his own profession. He is disdainful of the gadgets provided for him by Q Branch (regarding them as irrelevant and useless). He is still attractive to women—there's a toe-curling part where Ariadne fantasizes about what she'd like him to do to her—and he does become involved with the KGB agent, even though he recognizes the dangers inherent in the relationship.

# JAMES BOND: THE AUTHORIZED BIOGRAPHY OF 007

Ian Fleming's biographer, John Pearson, was the next to tackle Bond's adventures in print, although his book, *James Bond: The Authorized Biography of 007*, was rather different from anything that preceded or followed it. Built around the conceit that Fleming had been hired by the British Secret Service to write his stories in an effort to put SMERSH off the track of the real James Bond, it purports to tell Bond's story, picking up on the hint in the obituary in *You Only Live Twice* that there were "sensational novels" based on Bond's life. Some of the Fleming stories, therefore, were accounts of actual missions—such as *Casino Royale* or *Dr. No* (the "real" Bond is living with that story's heroine, Honey Rider, when Pearson meets him)—while others, notably *Moonraker*, were products of Fleming allowing his imagination full rein.

Pearson's Bond has "an air of tension" surrounding him, and he is clearly not overly happy about coming out from the shadows for Pearson's proposed official biography. During their discussions, many other sides to the character are revealed: he considered working as a store detective at one point, and he spent time living off his looks as a companion to wealthy women in island communities. He's been hurt on many occasions, and there were a number of influences in his life that helped shape him into the blunt instrument of the Secret Service—including Ian Fleming himself, during World War II.

The book concludes with the aging Bond (he's now in his fifties, so well past mandatory retirement age) heading out on a mission to Australia potentially involving Blofeld's lover, Irma Bunt. It wasn't an official Glidrose publication, and many of its details have been contradicted by later novels. However, as with Sean Connery's comeback film, *Never Say Never Again*, it provides an intriguing insight into how an older, more mature Bond might appear.

# JAMES BOND, THE SPY WHO LOVED ME

They may have deviated considerably from their source texts, but the James Bond movies were still ostensibly based on the stories by Ian Fleming. However, since Fleming had insisted that only the title of *The Spy Who Loved Me* could be used for

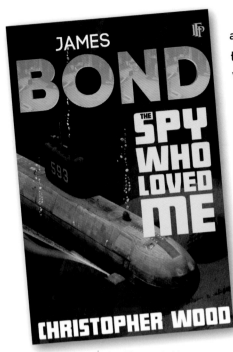

*Ian Fleming Publications' cover for the ebook reissue of Christopher Wood's novel makes no mention of its big screen origins.*

any film version, a complete new storyline was needed. While the eventual screenplay by Richard Maibaum and Christopher Wood bore some resemblance to Amis's *Colonel Sun*, as well as Roald Dahl's screenplay for *You Only Live Twice*, it was the first completely new Bond story for nearly a decade, and EON Productions authorized Wood to pen a novelization. This came under the control of Glidrose, owners of the Bond literary franchise, as did Wood's novelization of the next film, *Moonraker*.

However, where *James Bond and Moonraker* was a straightforward transcription of the plot into prose form, and does little to provide insight into Bond beyond formalizing the way in which Roger Moore played him on screen, *James Bond, The Spy Who Loved Me* is one of the better continuation novels. Wood consciously tries to tie it into Fleming's stories—when he is drugged, Bond berates himself for not remembering Rosa Klebb's machinations, for example—and returns SMERSH to action, under the control of Colonel-General Nikitin, a character featured in *From Russia, with Love*. "I re-read several Fleming Bonds in order to try and replicate the style," Wood recalled in 2005. "I wanted to do the man justice . . . I hope [the book] is more character-driven than the movie." He also commented: "It was a real challenge to integrate the extraordinary world of film Bond into the more prosaic, real-life settings of the novels."

While constrained to an extent by Roger Moore's screen persona (making 007 more prone to quips than the original character), this is a Bond who still smokes the triple-ringed Balkan/Turkish mixture cigarettes made for him at Morlands of Grosvenor Street, but who is aware that he's smoking far too much. He also acknowledges that he's at "the upper level of what a man could decently drink without being considered to have an overreliance on alcohol." He's got a good working knowledge of the current strengths and weaknesses of the British Navy (in a "card index in his mind"), and, luckily for him, he remembers the Latin name of a fish that was owned by one of his school friends. He is happy to use Q Branch's gadgets, particularly when they save his life, and feels more alive once a mission begins—although he hates the feeling of impotence when he can't control a situation. He can resist torture, as demonstrated in a brutal sequence that doesn't appear in the film (Wood called it a homage to *Casino Royale*), by focusing on the items around him, and he can be a cruel lover ("He came down on her like a hawk," we learn).

It would have been very interesting to see a complete original Bond novel from Christopher Wood that was not linked to the requirements of a blockbuster motion-picture screenplay.

## LICENCE RENEWED

Looking back, some years after he had finished writing the Bond continuation novels, famed British spy novelist John Gardner explained his original take on 007, after he was approached by Glidrose to revive James Bond for a new series of novels.

"What I wanted to do was take the character and bring Fleming's Bond into the 1980s as the same man, but with all he would have learned had he lived through the 1960s and 1970s . . . I wanted to put Bond to sleep where Fleming had left him in the 60s, waking him up now in the 80s having made sure he had not aged, but had accumulated modern thinking on the question of Intelligence and Security matters."

When he pitched this idea to the Glidrose board, they gave "what I can only describe as a corporate beam" and indicated that this fit with their plans. Gardner wanted to allow Bond to change—an idea that didn't always go down well with reviewers, if not readers—and he also wanted to ensure that he wouldn't have to "stay firmly within the painted lines of the original." Fleming had tried various experiments with his Bond stories—not just the poorly received *The Spy Who Loved Me*, but Bond's marriage, widowing and subsequent descent into despair—and Gardner wanted to do the same. It's fair to say that of all the continuation writers—bar Jeffery Deaver, whose situation was somewhat different since he was effectively reintroducing the character from scratch—Gardner was the only one to show Bond maturing and growing.

Gardner's first story, *Licence Renewed*, published in 1981, sets out his stall for 007. At least in this first story, he's Fleming's Bond, who, despite not having been cryogenically frozen and revived—*à la* Marvel's Captain America—has transferred his attitudes intact from 1964 to 1981. Over that time, however, his alcohol intake has reduced dramatically, and he has switched to smoking cigarettes made from a special low-tar brand of his favorite tobacco, still obtained from the same store, Morlands of Grosvenor Street, with their distinctive three rings, which he keeps in the same cigarette case that saved his life in *From Russia, with Love*.

He is just starting to show a few gray hairs, and Gardner cleverly circumvents Fleming's dictum about OO agents retiring at the age of 45 by disbanding the OO section altogether two years before the book opens. Bond—still nostalgically referred to as OO7 by M—is now a "blunt instrument" and one of M's executive officers. He doesn't have his own secretary anymore, and has a very flirtatious relationship with Miss Moneypenny (one of Gardner's few nods to the film incarnation). While he still respects M, there's far more rapport between them than seen previously, and his friendship with Bill Tanner is stronger than ever.

Bond still enjoys driving a top-class fast car, and now has a SAAB 900 Turbo, complete with various modifications. He no longer carries a Walther PPK after one failed during the (real-life) attempted kidnapping of Princess Anne in 1974; during the course of the first three books he tries various weapons. He has a cottage near Haslemere in Surrey, near to the "Sadist School" training center in Camberley, and he admits to having been a devotee of popular music while at school (although Gardner carefully doesn't give a decade). He's become a connoisseur of high fashion. He doesn't have a problem with Q Branch's gadgets, using one to help infiltrate the villain's headquarters, and he starts to develop a friendship with Ann Reilly, Major Boothroyd's assistant, who unfortunately is given the nickname Q'ute. (This follows what seems to be a typical 1960s seduction scene that plays out differently to how either Bond or the reader expects.) He now carries out a series of karate exercises each morning.

Some things don't change at all throughout Gardner's run on the books: Bond is capable of withstanding considerably more torture and pain than the ordinary man (on average, once a book), and the ladies persist in falling for his charms. Other peripheral items do alter quite soon: for example, Bond finds a new cigarette supplier in the second book, *For Special Services*. The daughters of Felix Leiter, Cedar, and Blofeld, Nena, both debut in this, with Bond falling for the single-breasted charms of the latter, while he's determined to avoid the advances of the former because of his friendship with her father—a side to OO7 we've not seen before.

In *Icebreaker*, one of Gardner's strongest entries, Bond teams up with CIA, KGB, and Mossad agents to battle the National Socialist Action Army, and becomes caught up in a series of double- and triple-crosses. Bond's literary tastes now include Eric Ambler (the author of *Epitaph for a Spy*), and he has an interest in sailing and jazz. His dreams feature memories of Royale-les-Eaux, both from when he visited it as a boy and from his encounter with Le Chiffre in *Casino Royale*; he also still has nightmares about his wife Tracy's death—something which comes to feature heavily in Gardner's Bond tales, and contrasts with the way in which Fleming had Bond move on in *The Man with the Golden Gun*. Although Gardner hinted at various missions that Bond carried out during the "missing years," *Icebreaker* marks the first time he's linked to a genuine historical event outside of World War II—we are told that he was active during the Falklands War in 1982, and even made a brief appearance on television.

We learn something about Bond's extended family in 1984's *Role of Honor*—James had an uncle Bruce, his father's brother, in Australia, who left him sufficient money in his will to buy a Bentley Mulsanne Turbo. (M suggested that James Bond had "so far as I am aware, no relative living" in *You Only Live Twice*, giving Gardner a small loophole to exploit.) Bond doesn't react well to boredom, and that combined with his profligate ways when he receives the legacy make him appear a security risk to the Americans—an attitude that M uses to set Bond up as bait for foreign agents, which eventually leads him to a revived SPECTRE. Under a new leader, Tamil Rahani, they plague Bond in the next book as well, *Nobody Lives For Ever*, in which Bond's mistrust of "people of short stature, knowing their tendency to overcompensate with ruthless pushiness" is made evident. (His lack of tolerance of homosexuals resurfaced in *Role of Honor*.)

Little of note is revealed about 007 in *No Deals, Mr. Bond*, published two years later, apart from M's belief that James isn't a fan of poetry and wouldn't "recognize Betjeman from Larkin," but in its successor, *Scorpius*, James remarries. However, both he and IRS agent Harriett Horner know that it's not a valid ceremony, given that it's carried out by arms dealer Vladimir Scorpius, claiming to be Father Valentine, head of the Society of Meek Ones. That, of course, doesn't stop 007 from consummating the marriage. ("We might as well get something out of this," Bond tells Harriett.) He's widowed again shortly afterwards, as he and Harriett try to escape.

## ENTER CAPTAIN BOND

Gardner's biggest change to 007 occurs in the 1989 novel *Win, Lose or Die*. Bond receives a promotion to the rank of captain when he is reassigned back to the Royal Navy, in an effort to prevent BAST (the Brotherhood for Anarchy and Secret Terror) disrupting a high-level secret conference between leaders Margaret Thatcher, George Bush, and Mikhail Gorbachev (all of whom Bond meets). For the remainder of Gardner's tales, 007 is referred to as "Captain Bond." We learn that he qualified as a naval pilot before joining the Secret Service, and maintained his flying hours and instrument ratings on both jets and helicopters while within the service, something which further deviates Gardner's Bond from the original character—there has been no mention of this at any stage previously. (This novel also rewrites M's personal history, giving the bachelor of *OHMSS* a daughter and grandchildren.) Bond shares the superstitions of many sailors, thinking that having women on a naval vessel is "bad luck." He's also not keen on "young women with either loud voices or runaway tongues" but does fall for Beatrice Maria da Ricci, whom he mourns deeply when he believes she's been killed.

*Brokenclaw*, which followed Gardner's adaptation of the second Timothy Dalton movie, *Licence to Kill* (in which the author can hardly hide his contempt for some of the errors in the plot), shows Bond's superstitions about quoting from Shakespeare's *Macbeth*, as well as his new ability to lip-read. It also claims that he lost his virginity at the age of fourteen—contradicting Fleming's description in "From a View to a Kill" that James was sixteen. Although Bond's ability to resist pain is undiminished, he is severely physically traumatized by the torture in this book at the hands of Chinese intelligence agent Lee Fu-Chu. We learn later, in *The Man from Barbarossa*, that it takes Bond a year to recover from the ordeal.

It's worth noting that by the time *The Man from Barbarossa* was published in 1991, Gardner is clearly keeping Bond's age magically in the mid-forties, despite the fact that he has been writing about him for nearly a decade, much of which has elapsed in real time in the stories (*Win, Lose or Die* covers a period of nine months, for example). Events in the 1960s are now meant to be before Bond's time, even if his assignments from that period and before definitely still happened—but either Bond or, more likely, Gardner has a blind spot regarding some of those previous adventures. Ironically, Gardner regarded *The Man from Barbarossa* as one of his best books, claiming that the American publishers "screamed in agony"

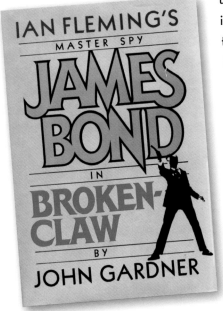

The cover from the hardback US edition of Brokenclaw, first published in 1990.

since it wasn't "the mixture as before." It is, though: *The Man from Barbarossa* is a retread of *Icebreaker*, down to the teaming up with other agents and the location of the villains' headquarters. Bond's knowledge of poetry is equally fickle: he quotes Dante and Eliot in earlier books, but here once again poetry is not his forte (nor is it M's now, contradicting *No Deals, Mr. Bond*)—yet in the next book, *Death is Forever*, Bond is quoting Eliot again.

Bond is given the Order of Lenin on the orders of President Gorbachev in *The Man from Barbarossa*; he turns down a knighthood in 1992's *Death is Forever*, but is awarded the Croix de Guerre by the French, after saving the lives of John Major, Helmut Kohl, François Mitterrand, and the other European Community leaders when a special train going through the Channel Tunnel is hijacked with them on board. *Death is Forever* reworks elements from *No Deals, Mr. Bond*, and we learn of Bond's dislike of weeping women—he compares them with having his teeth drilled, and seeing it makes him "cringe."

*Never Send Flowers* is the first part of a loose trilogy of adventures marking the end of John Gardner's tenure as Bond author. The final volume, *COLD* (aka *Cold Fall* in the US), was published after his novelization of *GoldenEye*, but Gardner very specifically sets up the arrival of the female M first seen in that story and charts the deterioration of the original M in the preceding tales. *Never Send Flowers* introduces Fredericka "Flicka" von Grüsse, a Swiss agent with whom Bond falls in love, as heavily as he did for Tracy in *OHMSS*. Bond and Flicka team up to prevent further assassinations, including an attempt on Princess Diana and her young sons when they visit Euro Disney. Bond (who apparently enjoyed Disney World—not something you'd expect from Ian Fleming's agent) confirms that he is an only child, and studied classic Greek literature (Aristophanes's *The Frogs*) at school.

Bond and Flicka continue to work together in Gardner's penultimate original novel, *Seafire*, which eliminates the 00 section (it had returned as an anti-terrorist unit earlier in Gardner's tenure) with a new Two Zeroes department, which answers to the MicroGlobe One intelligence watch committee, rather than to M. Bond now has a secretary with the unlikely name of Chastity Vain.

Bond asks Flicka to marry him, but she is captured and tortured by millionaire arms supplier Sir Maxwell Tarn at the end of *Seafire*, and in *COLD* (in which von Grüsse's nickname changes from Flicka to Freddie) she dies from her injuries, after

Bond has spent several months looking after her in between work missions. *COLD* is a real oddity in the Bond canon: it's divided into two parts, the first of which is set in 1990 (according to the US editions of the book, but this causes major continuity errors), around four years before *Seafire*, and then picks up immediately from the end of that story. Bond's artistic knowledge is on display: he can quote from both the Song of Solomon and the Book of Kings in the Bible; he's seen *The Wizard of Oz* and *Peter Pan*; and he once again quotes from T.S. Eliot. He had to learn one of Churchill's famous speeches from World War II—"this isn't the beginning of the end . . ."—at school (we have to assume Bond was born around 1950 for this to make sense). He's only truly loved four women: Tracy, Freddie/Flicka, and Beatrice da Ricci (who appeared in *Win, Lose or Die*) are named. The fourth is presumably Vesper Lynd from *Casino Royale*. He can't remember his father and has treated M as such—an interesting take on the relationship, particularly given the way that Daniel Craig's Bond reacts to his M, notably in *Skyfall*—and he wonders how he's going to react to his successor.

"If you don't at least try to take a new and different path and a truly creative approach in writing the Bonds they simply become flat, dull and unattractive," Gardner wrote in 2001. While some of his early work certainly added to our understanding of 007, his later books became pale imitations of themselves—and certainly not up to the standard of his own spy thrillers such as *The Secret Houses*, or his recreation of Sherlock Holmes's nemesis, James Moriarty. Gardner died in August 2007.

## BLAST FROM THE PAST

The mantle of Bond author fell on the shoulders of American writer Raymond Benson, a long-time fan of Ian Fleming's work, and the author of *The James Bond Bedside Companion*, an encyclopedic look at the whole 007 universe. During 1985 to 1986 he was a designer on the computer-game versions of *A View to a Kill* and *Goldfinger*, as well as a role-playing game, an original adventure *You Only Live Twice II: Back of Beyond*, and he penned an as yet unproduced stage version of *Casino Royale* for Glidrose. While he may not have written a novel before, he certainly knew his 007.

Benson's tales—six novels, three short stories, and novelizations of Pierce Brosnan's final three movies—appeared over a seven-year period and extended the literary Bond's spying career into the twenty-first century. His successors, with the exception of Jeffery Deaver, would embark on a process of "filling in the gaps" in Bond's history, setting their stories around previously published work, maintaining the fiction that they were still recounting the career of the Cold War agent introduced in *Casino Royale*. (Glidrose did consider getting Benson to do this, but eventually decided to keep moving forward.)

Benson was hired by Glidrose to succeed John Gardner in late 1995, after Gardner had delivered *COLD* and announced his retirement. His instructions were to keep M female, in line with the film series and Gardner's final story, and to "blend more contemporary elements (more action, gadgetry, humor) with the Bond character of the original books." Benson interpreted this as meaning to revert to the more politically incorrect and tough 007 created by Fleming; as he was at pains to point out, "every author's oeuvre of Bond novels should be taken as a whole and separate from other authors'—with the exception that Fleming's original books are the groundwork, the basis for the Universe." To Benson, Bond might be the "blunt instrument" referred to by Fleming, but he is also "very clever. Sharp and quick on his feet . . . I think he's a survivor who really knows how to survive . . . He's a machine; an animal." In his movie novelizations, Benson portrayed the Pierce Brosnan Bond; for his own stories, he imagined 007 as he appeared in the *Daily Express* newspaper strip.

"Blast from the Past" was Benson's debut 007 tale, a short story that appeared (in abbreviated form) in *Playboy* magazine in 1997. It gave a new perspective on Bond: he learned the fate of James Suzuki, the son he had fathered by Kissy Suzuki in *You Only Live Twice* and with whom he had kept in touch over the succeeding years. Because of the legal restrictions (EON owned the rights to all offspring of Bond), James Suzuki couldn't appear as a live character in the story, so Benson made this tale about 007 discovering that he is dead, and tracking down the woman responsible: Irma Bunt, the murderer of his wife, Tracy. There's no attempt made to explain how Bond can have a son in his twenties and still be in the

*Raymond Benson's six original novels that brought James Bond into the twenty-first century.*

mid-forties that he was at the time of his conception. The same problem plagues Benson's 1999 short story "Midsummer Night's Doom," in which Bond recalls meeting Donna Michelle, a Playmate of the Month from December 1963, the first time he encounters Hugh Hefner.

Benson opens the tale with Bond in bed with the 19-year-old "niece" of his housekeeper May (who herself must be heading for her century in age), thinking about some of the other women with whom he sleeps periodically—although "none had touched his heart in the way Tracy did." Bond's womanizing continues throughout Benson's stories—at least until *Never Dream of Dying*, when the author felt it was time for Bond to fall in love again, and introduced actress and model Tylyn Mignonne. This generated some controversy when Benson decided to show some of Bond's sexual techniques and was accordingly more explicit in the sex scenes, making reference to Tylyn's clitoris in a scene where Bond manually stimulates her; there were similar complaints when Pierce Brosnan's Bond was seen giving oral sex in the roughly contemporary *Die Another Day*.

His Bond has returned to using the Walther PPK, and has reverted to "Commander Bond"—no explanation is given for the change in rank. It's not as if Benson was ignoring Gardner's alterations to the mythos: in his first novel, *Zero Minus Ten*, set against the background of the handover of Hong Kong in 1997, Bond thinks about a number of ladies from Gardner's adventures. He's starting to build a relationship with the new M—as are Moneypenny and Bill Tanner—and this female head is firmly back in charge of the SIS: MicroGlobe One, the watch committee, is no more. The repartee with Major Boothroyd (Benson was not allowed to call him Q) is deliberately reminiscent of the film series—Ann Reilly, "Q'ute," has vanished, never to be mentioned or seen again—with Bond returning to a tolerance of the gadgetry. By Benson's second book, *The Facts of Death*, Boothroyd is even saying, "Now pay attention, 007." Bond has a new private assistant, Helena Marksbury, and after her demise, he gains a male secretary, Nigel Smith.

As far as Bond's private life is concerned, he is back in the Chelsea apartment looked after by May that he has used for years, although he has also bought Ian Fleming's old house in Jamaica, renaming it Shamelady. He maintains the same sort of exercise regime in the mornings that he has adhered to for years, and continues to like his breakfast prepared in a very particular way. Benson is meticulous in returning Bond to his roots in this sort of area, as well as in his chauvinism: in *The Facts of Death*, Felix Leiter is very patronizing about women and Bond totally agrees with the assertion that they "are like stamps—the more you spit on them, the more they get attached to you." His prowess with languages continues to be displayed: he speaks Cantonese fluently, but his Mandarin isn't as strong; he can get by in Greek, and has spent time in that country; and he is supposedly fluent in Japanese (even if he uses the wrong honorific title when addressing women).

Bond's prowess as a mountaineer comes to the fore in Benson's third novel, his personal favorite, *High Time to Kill*, in which it is casually asserted that 007 has climbed Mount Everest and Mount Elbrus (the highest mountains in the world and Europe respectively). The book also reveals a longstanding rivalry with Group Captain Roland Marquis, stretching back to their schooldays at Eton, and introduces a new foe for Bond, "The Union," a group of mercenaries against whom Bond battles over the course of three books.

In his fourth novel, *Doubleshot*, Benson delves most deeply into Bond's psyche, during his recuperation from the head injury he sustains during *High Time to Kill*. Bond has a lesion on the brain, which leads to blackouts and a change in personality—to the extent that he becomes a valid murder suspect. The story also shines a spotlight on Bond's domestic life more than previous novels, with Benson providing sufficient clues to pinpoint the address of Bond's Chelsea apartment.

The Union trilogy concludes with *Never Dream of Dying*, which throws an interesting light on a relationship often overlooked by Bond fans—between 007 and his former father-in-law, Marc-Ange Draco, the Unione Corse leader. Benson reasoned that Draco would have hated Bond for causing his daughter's death in *OHMSS*, and pits the two men against each other. "What I did with Draco was perfectly reasonable, given his character as Fleming created him," Benson pointed out. Bond is horrified to learn that family members are involved with the Unione, although this doesn't stop him disposing of them.

Benson's final Bond novel, *The Man with the Red Tattoo*, returns 007 to Japan, where he meets an old friend, Tiger Tanaka. The author had hoped to continue with the stories after a year's break, but Ian Fleming Publications (IFP—the successors to Glidrose) had other ideas.

# THE MONEYPENNY DIARIES

The events of 9/11 changed the world forever, revealing a very different sort of threat to world peace. Using a relic of the Cold War in novels set in a very different espionage environment might have been difficult, so IFP went a different route: they commissioned Charlie Higson to chronicle Bond's early years, detailed later in this chapter, and they presented a very different perspective on 007 in Samantha Weinberg's trilogy of novels and short stories about Miss Moneypenny.

*Samantha Weinberg, aka Kate Westbrook, discusses her work on The Moneypenny Diaries series.*

Written under the pseudonym "Kate Westbrook," supposedly Jane Moneypenny's niece, *The Moneypenny Diaries* were the first novels to be set between other writers' tales of Bond (Benson's short story "Live at Five" contains a flashback to the mid-Gardner era). The first book, *Guardian Angel*, shows us a Bond recovering from the events of *OHMSS*, and shows his and Moneypenny's involvement in the real-life Cuban Missile Crisis. Weinberg tried to stay true to the spirit of Fleming's creation, particularly the depression that Fleming refers to in *You Only Live Twice*, and explained the fates of some of Bond's former girlfriends. In the first book, she suggested that "Bond" wasn't the character's true name; she backpedaled on the idea in later stories.

The second book, *Secret Servant*, continues Weinberg's attempts to ground the Bond stories in the world of the real Secret Service as MI6 tries to cope with Kim Philby's defection and Bond's disappearance and return (as chronicled in *The Man with the Golden Gun*). *Final Fling* charts Bond and Moneypenny's attempts to find a traitor, known as the Sieve, within the service. This is paralleled with Kate Westbrook's investigation into her aunt's murder—in which she is helped by friends from the past.

# DEVIL MAY CARE

*Final Fling* appeared in 2008, to mark the centenary of Ian Fleming's birth. It wasn't the only new Bond novel that year: *Devil May Care* by "Sebastian Faulks, writing as Ian Fleming," continued the Bond saga of the 1960s, set in 1967 as 007 is still recovering from the death of Tracy. Faulks very consciously modeled his writing style on Fleming's for the book, and his Bond is Fleming's agent, enjoying alternately hot and cold showers, and displaying a cruelty that was softened in some of the other continuation novels. He drinks and smokes as much as he did in the original stories, and Faulks wanted to show a "very vulnerable man, with his nice suit and soft shoes and ludicrously underpowered gun. He finds himself in terrible situations, and he's all on his own—you just worry for his safety." Faulks admitted that the hardest part of writing *Devil May Care* was "writing about characters with hardly any interior life," noting that while Fleming provided "five percent of the hinterland behind the man," he was able to double that—but still not to the extent that he was accustomed to in his original fiction.

*Author Sebastian Faulks, the first writer to insert new adventures into James Bond's continuity, with his 2008 novel Devil May Care.*

# CARTE BLANCHE

After Faulks turned down the opportunity to pen a further novel, American thriller writer Jeffery Deaver was approached, only agreeing on the condition that he was allowed to present a contemporary take on Bond. In *Carte Blanche*, Deaver's Bond is Fleming's character reworked for the twenty-first century: physically he's the same, and he has many of the same characteristics, enjoying his alcohol and his food, dressing conservatively but stylishly. He doesn't smoke anymore, and is adept with all manner of gadgetry. Given that this was a similar makeover to the character that occurred on screen in *Casino Royale*, it's perhaps surprising that *Carte Blanche* wasn't better received.

# SOLO

William Boyd's *Solo*, like Weinberg's and Faulks's novels, is set in the 1960s, specifically in 1969, starting on Bond's forty-fifth birthday—a time when he should retire from the 00 section, according to Fleming, although this isn't mentioned at all within the book (Boyd did cover it in an ersatz interview he wrote with Bond for a newspaper feature after this was commented on in reviews: "I don't think I'll be retiring, somehow," Bond tells him). Like Weinberg, Boyd tries to amalgamate Fleming's world with the dirty realities of espionage in the 1960s, with the CIA involved in unauthorized covert operations in states they felt were inimical to American interests. Boyd's Bond has the surface trappings of Fleming's agent, although he drinks and smokes even more than his creator portrayed, and he recalls his wartime experiences in post-D Day Normandy.

*Author William Boyd poses with a sealed copy of his Bond novel Solo alongside a Jensen FF Mark I that Bond drives in the story.*

# YOUNG BOND

When we first meet James Bond, in *Casino Royale*, we are told very little of his background. A certain amount was filled in—notably in the obituary for the character in *You Only Live Twice*—and this has formed the basis not only for the backstory of *Skyfall* (with some amendments), but for a series of very successful novels.

However, the first person to write about James Bond's childhood wasn't Ian Fleming: it was J.M. (Johanna) Harwood in the spoof short story "Some Are Born Great" for the magazine *Nursery World* in 1959. Harwood—who later went on to co-write the scripts for *Dr. No* and *From Russia with Love*—showed us a Bond whose prowess at cards was evident at a very young age.

M's obituary for Commander Bond, which appeared in *The Times*, provides a few details about James's upbringing. John Pearson's "biography" of Bond covered some of this period, although the book's primary focus was on James's later years, once he was involved with the British Secret Service. Bond also makes a cameo appearance as a teenager in Tim Heald's "biography" of another fictional spy, *The Avengers*' John Steed, which doesn't present the future 007 in a good light at all.

In 2003, Charlie Higson was best known for his work as a comic writer and actor on British television, and had recently overseen a reboot of the 1960s series *Randall & Hopkirk (Deceased)*—aka *My Partner the Ghost*—when he was approached to write a series of novels about Bond's formative years. Taking Fleming's original dating for Bond's birth (somewhere around 1920, rather than the revision to 1924 in *You Only Live Twice*), he picked up James's story shortly after the death of his parents. Fleming explained that Bond was raised by his aunt Charmian, and Higson fleshed the character of the aunt out into the sort of woman who would be able to deal with the headstrong young orphan.

*Young Bond author Charlie Higson, who explained exactly why James Bond was sent down from Eton.*

Described disparagingly by Bond continuation author John Gardner as "the last desperate attempt to draw in a new audience," the *Young Bond* series was originally going to be written by multiple authors, with Higson only starting the series off, in much the same way that Kingsley Amis was intended to be only the first person to use the "Robert Markham" pseudonym. However, Higson was eventually contracted for five novels and one short story (contained in *The Young Bond Dossier*), which appeared between 2005 and 2009. These covered a highly eventful period in Bond's life, with the character noticeably maturing across the books, as well as developing many of the interests that would become prominent in his appearances in Fleming's stories.

Higson's Bond is, of course, much younger than any of the versions of the character seen elsewhere. Over the course of the series he learns some of the traits of patience and self-control, which will become necessary to his future trade, and, in a move that some fans of the books found difficult to accept, encounters people whose ambitions are perhaps rather more out of the ordinary than you might expect a normal teenager to meet—including Lord Randolph Hellebore, Count Ugo Carnifex and the Millenaria, Sir John Charnage, and Dr. Friend, as well as secret agents from various nations.

"[Bond] is a loner who nevertheless makes friends easily," Higson explained. "He has a strong sense of right and wrong. He is brave and resourceful. And he is good at punching." He was keen not to make James a "mini, shrunk-down version of the super-cool Pierce Brosnan," but to show the process by which he went from an ordinary schoolboy to a "more cynical and hardened" character. In *Hurricane Gold*, he undergoes a hazardous and torturous sequence which definitely changes him. "He's put through all these tasks and tests, and it definitely makes him stronger, but it also kind of destroys his soul to a certain extent," Higson told John Cox in 2008. "He becomes that sort of damaged person that he is in the adult books. He's got this tough shell but a damaged interior."

There is plenty of foreshadowing of later events: among many others, Bond is lectured about "playing Red Indians" by Lord Hellebore, referenced by Le Chiffre in *Casino Royale*; he acquires his Bentley with the proceeds from wins at a casino; his skiing instruction with Hannes Oberhauser, mentioned in "Octopussy," is shown. Higson's stories end with Bond leaving Eton, after the author found a way to cheat the timeframe to allow more time for James's adventures than the two "halves" that Fleming mentioned.

It seemed as if Ian Fleming Publications had switched their attentions to further adventures of the adult Bond, although Higson's tales were adapted into graphic novels, and there were two accompanying online games, *Avenue of Death* and *The Shadow War*. However, in October 2013, prolific young adult author Steve Cole was announced as the author of four new adventures, with the first, *Shoot to Kill*, arriving in November 2014. "It was a daunting project to tackle," Cole said in an interview for this book. "I wanted to do both Fleming's Bond and Charlie's younger character justice, having admired and enjoyed both sets of novels, and I knew expectation would be high. But Fleming is the wellspring, and I considered that the sixth Bond novel was *Dr. No*, which was the first to be made in Hollywood. That suggested to me that the sixth *Young Bond* could also take James to Hollywood, albeit in a more literal way! It took a couple of drafts to grow comfortable with making my own voice dominant with *Shoot to Kill*, but then that is what the role of Bond, whether acting or scripting, demands. You have to do it your own way, or what's the point of your being there?"

*Young Bond* wasn't the first attempt to create a Bond tale for a younger audience. The rather unusual *The Adventures of James Bond Junior 003½* was penned by the pseudonymous R.D. Mascott in 1967. It featured Bond's nephew James—son of 007's brother David, a character with no basis in the Fleming stories—who gets in various scrapes. Oddly, everyone seems to know who his uncle is, and Bond himself makes a very brief appearance. It's been suggested that the book was linked to various attempts to launch a TV series around a younger version of Bond. The book itself was reasonably reviewed but no further stories appeared.

Another nephew of 007 appeared in the animated series *James Bond Jr.* This 65-episode cartoon show was based on the idea of younger relatives of key agents (Bond, Q, etc.) being trained at Warfield Academy, and dealing with the agents of SCUM (Saboteurs and Criminals United in Mayhem) who included a number of 007's old enemies—many of whom had died on screen! Successful enough to spawn a comic-book series, novelizations, and a line of toys, the show's primary claim to fame is the creation of General Ourumov, in charge of Russia's space-based weapons division—a character who subsequently appears in *GoldenEye*.

THE MOST RECENT author to take up the Bond assignment is *Foyle's War* creator Anthony Horowitz. *Trigger Mortis*, released in September 2015, derives part of its plot from "Murder on Wheels," one of the unused stories Ian Fleming devised for the proposed TV series in the mid-1950s, with "original material by Ian Fleming" acknowledged on the cover. The novel starts two weeks after the events of Fleming's *Goldfinger*, with Bond placed in the middle of the Soviet/American space race, as the United States prepares for a critical rocket launch. *Trigger Mortis* features the return of Pussy Galore, as well as new Bond Girl Jeopardy Lane, and a "sadistic, scheming Korean adversary hell-bent on vengeance" called Jai Seung Sin.

*Anthony Horowitz, creator of Foyle's War and teenage spy Alex Rider, whose new novel embroils Bond in the world of motor racing.*

"Bond's mission is to make sure a Russian plot to scupper Moss's race by forcing him to crash is intercepted . . . there's a fantastic race Bond gets involved in," Fleming's niece Lucy explained.

"It was always my intention to go back to the true Bond, which is to say, the Bond that Fleming created, and it was a fantastic bonus having some original, unseen material from the master to launch my story," Horowitz noted. "My aim was to make this the most authentic James Bond novel anyone could have written."

Fleming's template, created over sixty years ago, continues to inspire writers.

# THE GUNS

James Bond and his Walther PPK: as Russian crime boss Valentin Zukovsky (Robbie Coltrane) notes in Pierce Brosnan's first movie as 007, they're forever linked in the minds of audiences as well as Bond's allies and enemies. The secret agent has used a PPK in nearly all of the movies, and we even saw him being issued with the gun during that very first briefing with M in *Dr. No.* (Interesting side note: the service armorer who gives Bond the gun, Major Boothroyd, isn't portrayed by Desmond Llewelyn, who otherwise portrayed the service's quartermaster "Q" throughout the twentieth-century movies—the credit goes to Peter Burton.)

The Walther PPK isn't a new gun. It dates back over eighty years and was originally designed by Carl Walther in Germany in 1931. The gun is a compact 7.65mm semi-automatic, which was developed to be used as a concealed weapon by the undercover elements of the police—the PPK stands for Polizei Pistole Kriminal (Police Pistol Criminal). Used extensively in the 1930s and 1940s by the German military and police, it was the gun that Adolf Hitler used to take his own life.

Because the PPK is only 6.1 inches (155mm) long and weighs around 21 ounces (less than 600g), it's been adopted by many forces around the world. Described by its manufacturers now as a "statement of sophistication" with "an abundance of the cool factor," in part because of its strong association with the 007 series, the PPK has been copied and remodeled many times over the years.

Fleming gave Bond the gun on the advice of the real Geoffrey Boothroyd, a firearms expert from Scotland who wrote him to complain about Bond's "deplorable taste in weapons" in the first novels. Boothroyd suggested the PPK, and Fleming provided an excuse for the change of weapons at the end of *From Russia, with Love*, when 007's gun misfires. Bond was then issued with a PPK for the rest of Fleming's stories, supplementing it when appropriate. Most of Fleming's literary successors

*The Walther PPK—the gun most associated with James Bond 007.*

followed suit, although, when writing in 1980, John Gardner was conscious that a PPK belonging to the Royal Protection Squad had jammed during the attempted kidnap of Princess Anne in 1974, and therefore changed Bond's gun. Raymond Benson returned Bond to the PPK for situations where concealment was necessary, and both Sebastian Faulks and William Boyd, writing stories set in the 1960s, kept Bond armed with a PPK.

In the movies, Boothroyd points out that the PPK has a "delivery like a brick through a plate-glass window," recommending that Bond uses a Brausch silencer. It's the gun that 007 mainly trusts his life to throughout the official series of movies, and in *Skyfall*, the new Q (Ben Whishaw) provides a PPK/S, the 9mm version of the weapon, to replace the PPK that Bond throws away during the initial chase sequence after it has run out of ammunition.

The gun that Bond was forced to hand over in *Dr. No* (both book and film) was his trusted Beretta .25, a weapon Geoffrey Boothroyd told Fleming was "utterly useless as well as being a lady's gun, and not a very nice lady at that." The movie Boothroyd is as cutting: "Nice and light . . . in a lady's handbag."

The automatic Modelo 418 was introduced in the early 1940s by Fabbrica d'Armi Pietro Beretta, the latest version of the .25 caliber weapon they had first released after World War I, and the gun was used by the Italian military during World War II. It was designed for close-range use—it was only really effective up to around fifteen yards, compared with the PPK's twenty-five—and lacked the

*A Beretta 9mm Parabellum, similar to that used by Bond in his earliest literary adventures (derided as a "lady's gun" by the Secret Service armorer).*

necessary stopping power. After its replacement by the PPK, the Beretta wasn't mentioned in the books or the films (in fact, Bond hands over an earlier model of the Beretta in *Dr. No*), although Ursula Andress's Vesper Lynd does use one in the spoof Bond movie *Casino Royale*, and Roger Moore's 007 acquires one during the course of his investigations in *The Spy Who Loved Me*. Jim Lawrence returned it to 007 in the newspaper strips following *River of Death* in 1969.

The other weapon that 007 is officially given on more than one occasion in print and on film is the Walther P99, which was developed in the 1990s. It first appeared in *Tomorrow Never Dies*, when Bond borrows one from Chinese agent Wai Lin (Michelle Yeoh). He is then officially issued with the gun in the next three films in place of the PPK; Raymond Benson used the P99 alongside the PPK in his later novels, opting for the former when concealment wasn't necessary—the P99 is considerably more bulky than the PPK.

Bond does carry another gun on more than one mission: the ASP 9mm, which makes its debut in John Gardner's fourth novel, *Role of Honor*, after the author had experimented with different firearms prior to that and sought inspiration in the book *The Handgun*, by Geoffrey Boothroyd. The ASP (Armament System Protection) weapon was built by Paris Theodore, owner of Seventrees, Ltd., a custom gun shop in New York in the 1970s and 1980s, and was based on the Smith & Wesson Model 39. It was specifically designed not to snag on clothing when it was being drawn and had a special "guttersnipe" sight rather than the normal front gun-sight. When Jeffery Deaver rebooted Bond for his 2011 novel *Carte Blanche*, he equipped him

*Two rather special weapons: the Golden Gun (above) created for Christopher Lee to use as Scaramanga in* The Man with the Golden Gun, *and the Colt Python .357 Magnum (right) awarded to Ian Fleming "For Special Services" by the Colt Company in 1964.*

with a Walther PPS .40 S&W, a gun that was the product of both Walther and Smith & Wesson.

In Fleming's books, Bond was never far from a gun. He kept a long-barreled Colt Army Special .45 under the dashboard of his Bentley in Fleming's first three novels—it's in his Aston Martin in *Goldfinger*—and he also got to use it in the short story "From a View to a Kill." John Gardner updated his concealed weapon to a Ruger Super Blackhawk .44 Magnum, hidden in 007's Saab Turbo in *Licence Renewed*. Ever ready for action, Bond also often kept a gun—identified as a Colt Police Positive .38 with sawn barrel in *Casino Royale*—beneath his pillow!

# CHAPTER 005

# SEAN CONNERY: THE SCOTTISH BOND

T HE PATH JAMES BOND TOOK TO ARRIVE AT THE BIG SCREEN WAS TORTUROUS, BUT EVEN AFTER HARRY SALTZMAN AND ALBERT R. "CUBBY" BROCCOLI ACQUIRED THE RIGHTS TO ALL OF IAN FLEMING'S STORIES (BAR *CASINO ROYALE*) AND TEAMED UP TO CREATE EON PRODUCTIONS IN 1961, THERE WAS STILL A LONG WAY TO GO BEFORE THAT FIRST MOMENT WHEN BOND APPEARED ON SCREEN.

Once EON had decided to produce *Dr. No* as the first film—*Thunderball* was also considered, but the ongoing legal proceedings regarding the book's genesis put the producers off—they commissioned various screen treatments. Some of these were less serious than others: in one, penned by Wolf Mankowitz and Richard Maibaum, the villain was called "Buchfield," and Dr. No was the name of his pet capuchin monkey. In the end, Maibaum, Johanna Harwood, and Berkely Mather's script treated both the villain and his opponent seriously.

But who could play James Bond? According to Cubby Broccoli, Ian Fleming favored Roger Moore, soon to embark on a long stint playing Leslie Charteris's

OPPOSITE: *Sean Connery assumes his license to kill once more in 1983's Never Say Never Again.* **ABOVE:** *Albert Broccoli, director of three of the first four Bond movies, lines up a shot.*

Simon Templar on the British TV series *The Saint*. Cary Grant and Patrick McGoohan were considered, the latter turning the role down, as he had that of the Saint, because of his concerns about the character's morality. (He wasn't the only one; the Vatican would issue a communique denouncing the morality of the first film!) George Baker, Patrick Allen, Richard Burton, Michael Redgrave, Trevor Howard, and Richard Johnson were all debated and discarded. Male model Peter Anthony was screen tested. The readers of Britain's *Daily Express* newspaper—which had been running the comic-strip adaptation of Fleming's stories since 1958—were polled. Their answer matched EON's eventual decision: Scottish actor Sean Connery.

Born in 1930, Thomas Sean Connery had served in the Royal Navy, and then taken a number of blue-collar jobs, including milkman, truck driver, lifeguard at the public baths, and coffin polisher. He occasionally modeled for the Edinburgh College of Art, showing off his toned physique, which also helped him in a Mr. Universe contest, from which he gained some acting roles. The archetypal "tall, dark, and handsome" man— or so he was described by the *New York Times* when he took the lead in the Disney movie *Darby O'Gill and the Little People* in 1959—learned his new trade well, taking a well-received role opposite Claire Bloom in a BBC production of Tolstoy's *Anna Karenina*, which was fresh in the memory when EON came to cast *Dr. No*.

Although Connery seemed to have a lot of the necessary physicality of Bond, and a "cocksure animal magnetism," some of the key personnel involved had doubts. Certainly, not everyone was as impressed with Connery as Broccoli's wife, Dana. "Cubby, he's fabulous!" she told her husband when he wondered if Connery had the necessary sex appeal to play 007. Ian Fleming thought he was more like "an overgrown stunt man," although his then mistress disagreed; the writer eventually warmed to Connery so much that Bond's heritage in the books became part-Scottish!

Terence Young was hired to direct the first James Bond movie—he had worked with Sean Connery on the movie *Action of the Tiger*—and Connery modeled his performance on Young's distinctive methods and mannerisms. The first Miss Moneypenny, Lois Maxwell, recalled that "Terence took Sean under his wing. He took him to dinner, showed him how to walk, how to talk, even how to eat." Connery's absorption of Young's ways even led some members of the crew to believe that the actor was deliberately impersonating the director. Young was extreme in his methods at times: before filming began, he made Connery sleep in a Savile Row suit and tie so that he would look comfortable in such clothes at all times.

# DR. NO *(1962)*

In *Dr. No*, MI7's 007, James Bond, is assigned to look into the disappearance of Commander Strangways, the Secret Service's resident agent in Jamaica, which coincides with American rockets being "toppled" off course mysteriously. Bond teams up with CIA agent Felix Leiter (Jack Lord), and discovers that Strangways was investigating the island of Crab Key and its owner, Dr. No (Joseph Wiseman). When 007 visits Crab Key, he meets local fisher-girl Honey Rider (Ursula Andress), before they are captured by Dr. No, who is a scientific genius working for SPECTRE. Dr. No is responsible for the "accidents" to the US rockets, and Bond must escape from his cell and rescue Honey before killing Dr. No and preventing further catastrophe.

The Bond we meet in this first movie is rather more refined in some ways than his literary predecessor. He is a member of the exclusive Le Cercle, part of Les

The UK Quad poster for the first Bond film designed by Mitchell Hooks emphasized 007's prowess with the ladies.

Sean Connery .. James Bond 007
**Dr. No**

Sean Connery .. James Bond 007
**Dr. No**

Sean Connery .. James Bond 007
**Dr. No**

Ambassadeurs club in Mayfair (whereas Fleming's Bond would only visit such places if required to by his boss, M, played throughout Connery's tenure by Bernard Lee). He has a luxurious apartment nearby, and carries cards bearing its address; he also smokes cigarettes, which he takes from a gunmetal case. He knows his champagnes: he prefers the 1953 vintage Dom Pérignon over the 1955. He has had time available to follow his leisure pursuits recently: at the end of his previous mission, he was injured and spent six months in hospital recovering. He has a set of golf putters in his apartment.

He enjoys female company, making a strong impression on fellow card-player Sylvia Trench (Eunice Gayson), sleeping with Miss Taro (Zena Marshall), and being protective of Honey Rider when they are in Dr. No's headquarters. He has a flirtatious relationship with M's secretary, Miss Moneypenny, and is not above arguing with his boss, particularly when M insists on changing Bond's gun. He is an excellent shot: he claims that during the ten years he has been using a Beretta, he has never missed with it. He can be cold and calculating: one of the most cold-blooded moments in the Bond films comes when 007 allows Dr. No's agent Professor Dent to empty

*Lobby cards show three key moments from the first film: the audience's introduction to James Bond at the gambling table (top), his flirtation with Sylvia Trench (middle), and with Miss Moneypenny (bottom).*

his gun into what he believes is Bond's supine form, before he shoots him (twice in the final print; six times in the original script). He will kill when he needs to, but isn't fearless—he's reduced to vomiting after he manages to avoid being bitten by a poisonous tarantula (although Connery himself was really in no danger: there's a clear sheet of glass between the spider and his flesh!). He has a dry sense of humor, coming out with quips after various close calls.

# FROM RUSSIA WITH LOVE (1963)

Many of the same elements were present and correct in the second film, *From Russia with Love*, once again penned by Maibaum and Harwood and directed by Terence Young, which arrived in cinemas in 1963.

James Bond is the target of a sting operation by SPECTRE, who are after the Russians' new Lektor code-breaking machine and also want revenge for Dr. No's death. Young Russian agent Tatiana Romanova (Daniela Bianchi) is used as a pawn and told to offer the device to the British if Bond is sent to collect it. Bond arranges her defection, and is pursued across Europe by SPECTRE assassin Red Grant (Robert Shaw), who plans to frame Bond for Tatiana's murder and steal the Lektor. Bond turns the tables, and when Grant's boss, former KGB agent Rosa Klebb (Lotte Lenya), tries to kill him, Tatiana shoots her.

When in England, Bond drives a green Bentley, which has a phone within it that is connected to the Secret Service headquarters. He is now finding time to date Sylvia Trench ("an old case") after being away for six months; there's no mention of what has happened to Honey Rider. He has a scar on the small of his back, possibly from turning his back on the wrong woman, and enjoys golf. He knows the right wines to have with different dishes (which he realizes should have put him onto Grant's deception earlier). He continues to flirt with Miss Moneypenny, and seems perfectly capable of handling the demands of two gypsy girls when asked to decide an argument

**ABOVE:** *The UK Quad poster art by Eddie Paul and Renato Fratini was recently judged the best-ever 007 poster.* **LEFT AND BELOW:** *Lobby cards show Kerim Bey and Bond preparing to get revenge for the attack on the gypsy camp (left) and Bond enjoying some belly-dancing (below).*

between them. He lives up to Tatiana's expectations of him (well, she says she'll tell him if he does in the morning, and they're still together then!), and on the subject of "Western girls" he tells her that he had "an interesting experience" with M in Tokyo, which puts an intriguing slant on his relationship with his superior. (We don't hear more about that because M stops the recording before telling Moneypenny to leave the room.) He mocks Tatiana's superstitions about the date being the thirteenth.

Professionally, Bond doesn't know that much about cryptography, although he recognizes the value of the Lektor, and he doesn't think he's likely to need the "smart-looking piece of luggage" that Q Branch has "put together." He is perfectly capable of hurting a woman when necessary, and threatens to do worse if he's lied to; he keeps his cool under pressure, even when facing a psychopath with a gun, and is a capable fighter at close quarters, as he demonstrates against Grant.

# GOLDFINGER *(1964)*

The third Bond film, *Goldfinger*, was adapted by Richard Maibaum and Paul Dehn, with Guy Hamilton joining the team as director after negotiations broke down with Terence Young. Jack Lord was invited back to play Bond's CIA contact Felix Leiter, but wanted equal billing with Connery; he was replaced by Cec Linder. Honor Blackman became the first of the stars of the British TV series *The Avengers* to make an appearance in the Bond franchise: Diana Rigg and Joanna Lumley would both be seen in *OHMSS*, while Patrick Macnee guest starred in *A View to a Kill* (and his movie counterpart, Ralph Fiennes, debuted as Mallory in *Skyfall*).

After two films in which the heightened reality of the villains' plans and bases was largely counterpointed with the realism of the Secret Service, *Goldfinger* is where the films start to inhabit a world of their own. From Q Branch's well-equipped workshop, providing 007 with a gadget-laden Aston Martin, to Goldfinger's headquarters (let alone Fort Knox itself, which bore little resemblance to the real-life gold depository), the film lived up to its tagline: "Everything he touches turns to excitement."

On his way back through Miami from a mission, Bond is asked to check out Auric Goldfinger (Gert Frobe), and discovers he's a card cheat. After he "borrows" Goldfinger's girlfriend, he's knocked out, and the girl is killed by having her entire body painted with gold—the precious metal on which Goldfinger is fixated and is smuggling out of Britain. Bond follows him to Switzerland and is captured; after interrogation, he's brought to Goldfinger's stud farm in Kentucky, where he learns that Goldfinger intends to rob Fort Knox. Goldfinger has assembled a team whose equipment will get him in to the depository, but he kills the leaders then tells Bond he is actually going to irradiate the gold supply on behalf of the Red Chinese. After persuading Goldfinger's pilot, Pussy Galore, to switch sides so

**LEFT:** *The US 3 sheet movie poster (which is larger than traditional 1 sheet) for Goldfinger went for a photographic montage rather than the stylized artwork of the previous films.* **OPPOSITE AND ABOVE:** *Lobby cards show Bond with Pussy Galore and Goldfinger; and the raid on Fort Knox.*

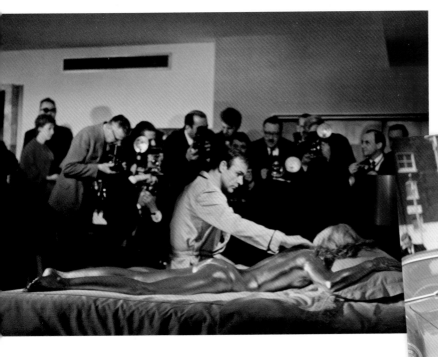

no lives are lost, Bond is able to kill Goldfinger's henchman, Oddjob (Harold Sakata), and then later dispose of Goldfinger.

With the change of director came a revised version of James Bond. The quips are more frequent—starting with, "Shocking, positively shocking," when he electrocutes an assassin at the start of the film—and the double entendres begin to creep in: "Something big's come up," Bond says (immodestly) when explaining why he's in bed with Jill Masterson (Shirley Eaton) rather than having dinner with Felix Leiter. His Bentley has "had its day," so he is provided with a new car, and far from believing that he won't need the gadgets Q provides, he listens moderately attentively to the briefing about the Aston Martin (we cut away before we learn if it lasts the full hour that Q threatens). He drinks his martinis shaken, not stirred, and is an expert on wines; however, now he is something of a show-off about his knowledge ("Colonel Smithers is giving the lecture," M has to remind him acidly). His alcohol intake is joked about by his friends (Leiter orders sufficient drinks for three for him on the plane taking Bond to the White House).

The relationship with Moneypenny continues as before, but M is definitely tetchier

with him—perhaps because Bond exceeded his orders with Goldfinger—and he warns Bond that 008 can replace him if Bond can't treat the assignment "coldly and objectively." Bond is a good golfer, playing off the same (unmentioned) handicap as Goldfinger.

He's still got the same keen eye for the ladies, dealing with some "unfinished business" in Mexico (the dancer, Bonita); dropping Dink, a young Miami lady, in favor of Jill Masterson, whom he seduces; trying to maintain some self-discipline when he first sees the attractive girl who turns out to be Tilly Masterson (Tania Mallet); and, of course, going for a roll in the hay with Pussy Galore. He's also a font of unusual knowledge: he knows the capabilities of the specific nerve gas Goldfinger plans to use, but he doesn't realize that all you have to do to defuse a Chinese-supplied nuclear device is flip a switch.

## THUNDERBALL *(1965)*

Terence Young returned for a final time to helm *Thunderball*, which was based on the screenplay *James Bond of the Secret Service* that Fleming had written with Kevin McClory and Jack Whittingham, as well as Fleming's later book. Both Guy Hamilton and Paul Dehn elected not to return for the new film, with the script finalized by Richard Maibaum and John Hopkins. The scope of the movie matched *Goldfinger*, with SPECTRE taking a larger, more central role in proceedings, and Bond becoming an ever larger-than-life character himself.

*Director Terence Young chats with his cast on the set of* Thunderball.

Bond is sent to a health farm to detox, but finds himself investigating the mysterious Count Lippe (Guy Doleman), who is in fact a SPECTRE agent in the middle of arranging the replacement of a NATO bomber pilot, Derval, with a lookalike so that SPECTRE can hijack a consignment of bombs. Bond becomes part of a global search for the weapons, and is sent to the Bahamas to question Derval's sister Domino (Claudine Auger).

Working once again with Felix Leiter (Rik van Nutter this time), he realizes that Domino's lover, Emilio Largo (Adolfo Celi), is involved with SPECTRE, and learns that the bombs are going to be moved from the crashed bomber onto Largo's boat. After a major underwater battle, Largo escapes with one bomb, but Bond intercepts him; Domino avenges her brother's death, killing Largo.

Bond undergoes treatment at Shrublands health spa. We don't know why he's there; no indication is given that it isn't voluntary, and it obviously isn't linked to the government, since SPECTRE are using it, and Bond describes himself as a "sort of licensed troubleshooter" to one of the staff. It's obviously the source of

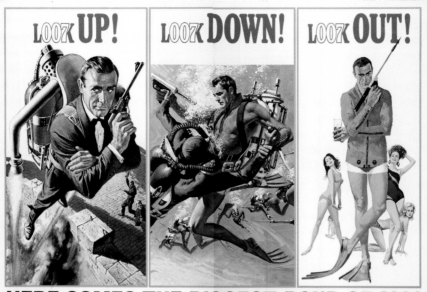

LOOK **UP!** LOOK **DOWN!** LOOK **OUT!**

HERE COMES THE BIGGEST BOND OF ALL!

ALBERT R. BROCCOLI and HARRY SALTZMAN present **SEAN CONNERY**

IAN FLEMING'S **"THUNDERBALL**

CLAUDINE AUGER · ADOLFO CELI · LUCIANA PALUZZI Produced by KEVIN McCLORY Directed by TERENCE YOUNG Screenplay by RICHARD MAIBAUM and JOH…
Based on an original story by KEVIN McCLORY, JACK WHITTINGHAM and IAN FLEMING PANAVISION® TECHNICOLOR® Released thru UNI…

*LEFT: Frank McCarthy and Robert McGinnis' original artwork for the Thunderball poster was heavily cropped for this unusual version.*
*BELOW: A portrait of SPECTRE agent Fiona, played by Luciana Paluzzi.*

some amusement at his expense—Moneypenny teases him about the weakening effects of the regime there.

His opinions are respected sufficiently by M to instantly back them over those of an RAF officer, and he isn't overly happy to see Q out in the field; Q isn't best pleased either, regarding Bond's attitude to his work as "frivolous." Certainly, the quips continue, with a tinge of black humor: "Mind if my friend sits this one out? She's just dead!" he comments after SPECTRE agent Fiona (Luciana Paluzzi) is shot.

Bond's card-playing skills are as sharp as ever, as is his enjoyment of female company, as he seduces the masseuse at Shrublands and tries to make an impression on Domino—

*A key battle of wits between 007 and Emilio Largo at the card table, as the duplicitous Fiona looks on.*

when he removes sea-egg spines from her feet, he claims, "It's the first time I've tasted women. They're rather good." He's an accomplished swimmer, even before he gets assistance from Q's various gadgets.

He tells Largo he knows "a little about women," but that he's "not what you call a passionate man"—although he rather proves the opposite with Fiona, who complains that he "made a shocking mess of [her] hair" and describes him as a "sadistic brute." He's not fooled by her, though: he spots that she wears the same ring as Largo, and keeps a gun under his pillow during that assignation in case she makes the wrong sort of move. He tells her that he made love to her "for King and country" and that it didn't give him any sort of pleasure; she responds by tweaking his ego.

## YOU ONLY LIVE TWICE (1967)

Sean Connery's fifth outing as 007 looked as if it would be his last. The part of Bond had made him a global superstar, with all the concomitant attention from the press—during the filming of *You Only Live Twice*, he was even pursued into the bathroom by persistent Japanese reporters—and he was becoming increasingly bored of the one-dimensional character of Bond, as he made abundantly clear in the few interviews that he gave. In one rare interview, with *Playboy* in November 1965, he explained that he was contracted for two further films after *Thunderball*, and if they wanted him back they'd have to pay a million dollars plus a percentage of the gross (compared with the roughly half a million dollars he earned for *Thunderball*). The increasingly

**LEFT:** *Ken Adam's incredible set for Blofeld's headquarters inside a volcano—built at Pinewood Studios.* **BELOW:** *An aerial shot of Pinewood Studios in 1967 during the filming of You Only Live Twice.* **BOTTOM:** *The black office chair used by villain Ernst Stavro Blofeld in You Only Live Twice. It was auctioned at Julien's for $16,250.*

fractious relationship between star and producers led to *You Only Live Twice* becoming—as far as everyone was concerned at the time—Connery's farewell.

Roald Dahl penned the final screenplay based on story elements created by Harold Jack Bloom, and later commented on the formulaic elements that went into the process. He jettisoned the majority of Fleming's plot and its concentration on revenge—this might well not have happened had *OHMSS* been filmed following *Thunderball* as was originally planned—instead reviving SPECTRE's fascination with rockets, as seen in *Dr. No*. Dahl's *You Only Live Twice* is the source of many of the features commonly attributed to Bond films: the physically deformed madman with his lair at the heart of a volcano, sitting stroking his white cat, as James Bond saves the day. Mike Myers's Dr. Evil in the Austin Powers films is an affectionate tribute, and there are many sequences within Myers's films that reference this particular Bond film. Lewis Gilbert made his debut as director.

After faking his own death (he's shot while in bed with a beautiful woman), James Bond is sent to Japan to investigate the disappearance of an American spacecraft. In Tokyo he works with the Japanese Secret Service leader Tiger Tanaka (Tetsurō Tamba) to uncover a plot by Blofeld (Donald Pleasence—the first time the character is properly seen on

screen)—and SPECTRE to try to trigger a nuclear war between the US and the USSR by hijacking their rockets. Bond and Tanaka's people follow a shipment of rocket fuel from Osato Chemicals, which leads them to Blofeld's base. Disguised as a ninja, 007 infiltrates it, and is able to make Blofeld's super rocket self-destruct before it can commit another hijacking.

Although there's no proper equivalent of Bond's obituary from the book in the film version of *You Only Live Twice* (that had to wait for *Skyfall*), we do learn something about his past—rather surprisingly, he got "a first in Oriental Languages at Cambridge," the first hint that Bond is a university graduate. We also see him in naval uniform. He accepts a martini "stirred, not shaken" from local MI6 agent Dikko Henderson (Charles Gray) without complaint, and can

**ABOVE:** *Robert McGinnis and Frank McCarthy's US poster for Connery's fifth outing, emphasizing to audiences that this was the real James Bond.*
**RIGHT:** *A selection of toys released to tie in with* You Only Live Twice, *including Bond's gyrocopter "Little Nellie."*

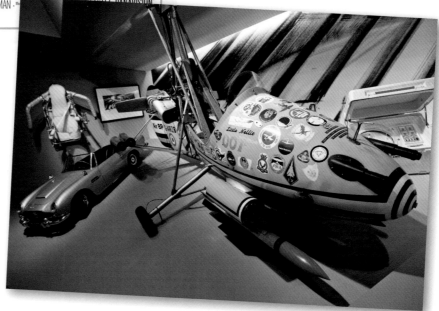

tell instantly that it's proper Russian vodka (he takes a swig of Siamese vodka later and clearly regrets it). He is aware of the correct way to serve and drink sake, which makes him seem very cultivated for a European. Interestingly, he claims that he's never been to Japan before, although he's talking to Henderson at this point and could be deliberately not making reference to his trip to the country with M mentioned in *From Russia with Love*.

Bond's propensity for liking a pretty face is known to other intelligence agencies—Tanaka is "a trifle disappointed" that Bond will "get into anything with any girl." He's very taken with the Japanese attitude toward women that Tanaka demonstrates ("men always come first"), and is happy to allow Japanese agent Aki (Akiko Wakabayashi) to "serve under" him. He's now something of a connoisseur of different women's tastes. To save his life, he makes love to Mr. Osato's assistant, Helga (Karin Dor)—"The things I do for England," he quips—then lies about it to Aki to save her from being too shocked. He has a hairy chest—which is showing signs of damage from his cigarette smoking, according to Mr. Osato's X-ray machine. Tanaka also comments on his excess smoking.

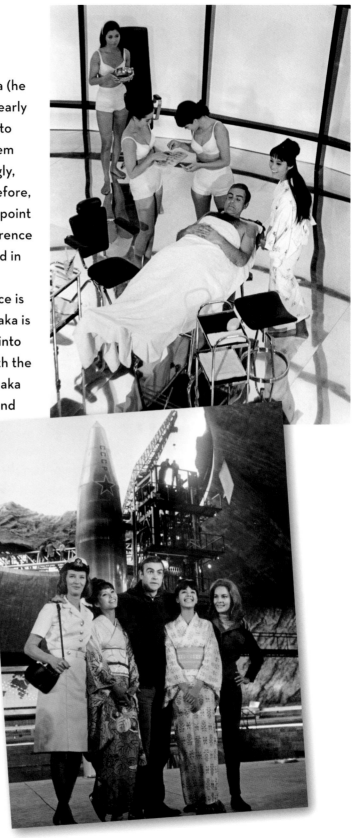

**ABOVE RIGHT:** *Preparing to film the scene where James Bond is turned into a Japanese ninja.* **RIGHT:** *Sean Connery with his female co-stars on the volcano set of You Only Live Twice.*

Although his interaction with M is more respectful than in recent films, his attitude to Q is as barbed as ever—and the quartermaster is "in no mood for your juvenile quips." He's used "Little Nellie"—the gyrocopter Q has brought to Japan—before, and apparently he's the only agent armed with a Walther PPK (well, that's what Blofeld says, anyway). Although he is an accomplished fighter, he is given ninja training by Tanaka's men. It may seem as if he intends to try to pilot the SPECTRE spacecraft, but in fact he's simply replacing one of Blofeld's men, presumably to do something to the others en route into space. However, he is spotted before he can proceed, and meets Blofeld for the first time.

## DIAMONDS ARE FOREVER *(1971)*

Sean Connery was adamant that he wouldn't return after the end of *You Only Live Twice*, and so Bond was played by George Lazenby in *OHMSS* (see next chapter). However, Connery would be persuaded back into the Secret Service for two further missions.

Lazenby unwisely followed the advice he was given not to sign up for more than one Bond film, and between his unwillingness and the problems with his behavior on set, it was clear that a new 007 was needed for *Diamonds Are Forever*. American actor John Gavin was contracted to play the role, but then Connery agreed terms (a hefty fee and profit participation that went to charity; an equally hefty overrun fine; and United Artists' agreement to support two other films Connery wanted to make). Gavin was speedily paid off, and Connery strolled back into the part, working once more with his *Goldfinger* director Guy Hamilton—a conscious attempt by EON to replicate that movie's success. The script by Richard Maibaum and Tom Mankiewicz uses Fleming's character names and his diamond-smuggling plot as a springboard for yet another space-based caper for SPECTRE.

Bond gets revenge on Blofeld (now played by Charles Gray) for Tracy's death (at the end of *OHMSS*), killing the SPECTRE leader as he prepares a load of body-double duplicates. Returning to work, 007 is put onto a gang of diamond smugglers, and he follows the pipeline through which the criminals transport their goods with the initially unwitting help of smuggler Tiffany Case (Jill St. John), as well as covert assistance from Felix Leiter (this time portrayed by Norman Burton).

*Sean Connery .. James Bond 007 ..*
**"Diamonds Are Forever"**

*Sean Connery .. James Bond 007 ..*
**"Diamonds Are Forever"**

*Sean Connery .. James Bond 007 ..*
**"Diamonds Are Forever"**

*ABOVE: Robert McGinnis' artwork for the 1971
movie poster emphasizes Connery's return—but
gives only tiny recognition to Bond's creator.
LEFT: Lobby cards show Bond's arrival in
Willard Whyte's penthouse (top); 007 on Sunset
Strip (middle); and relaxing with Tiffany Case
(bottom).*

This leads them to a research center belonging to reclusive millionaire Willard Whyte (Jimmy Dean), where a laser is being built using the diamonds, which is sent into orbit. It also leads to Whyte's penthouse, where Bond learns that Blofeld is not dead. Bond tracks Blofeld to his base on an oil rig, from where he is using the satellite to destroy nuclear weapons before he proposes to auction nuclear supremacy. During an attack on the rig, Bond uses Blofeld's own escape craft to cause the satellite control to be destroyed.

*ABOVE: Time for some light reading and a martini or two for Connery's Bond.*
*LEFT: Sean Connery and Jill St. John relax during the filming of Diamonds Are Forever.*

Although it's fair to say that Bond is driven by revenge at the start of the film, doing whatever's necessary to get on Blofeld's trail, he's back to his wise-cracking, womanizing self pretty quickly once he's disposed of his nemesis. When he realizes the villain isn't dead, meeting him both in Whyte's penthouse and later at the oil rig, the foes exchange quips—there's little sign that Bond feels burning hatred toward the man whose actions robbed him of his wife. Initially posing as Peter Franks, 007 flirts with Tiffany Case, and he can't resist a joke about Las Vegas good-time girl Plenty O'Toole's name.

His wine-recognizing skills irritate M (although the byplay between them when M tries to rebuke him for ascribing a year to sherry wasn't in Mankiewicz's original script), but he doesn't know much about diamonds, to M's evident relief. He's a member of the Playboy Club (membership number 40401).

After his fake death in *You Only Live Twice* to put old enemies off his scent, clearly everyone knows

*Behind the scenes on Diamonds Are Forever as Sean Connery and Jill St. John prepare to shoot a scene with Bambi and Thumper.*

that Bond has resurfaced: even Tiffany Case, a smuggler who would normally not have anything to do with the Secret Service, is aware of who he is and what a big deal it is to kill him. Given that she works for Blofeld indirectly, it is possible that all SPECTRE agents were told to keep an eye out for him—but, in reality, this marks the start of the contradiction that characterizes the 1970s' Bond: the secret agent whom everyone knows.

# *NEVER SAY NEVER AGAIN* *(1983)*

Connery was adamant that he was only returning for one film, and the part was taken for the rest of the decade by Roger Moore. Kevin McClory had never given up his dream of remaking *Thunderball*, and Connery became involved with the maverick producer both on an abortive 1976 version, *Warhead*, and then with *Never Say Never Again*, the movie that went head to head with Moore's sixth screen outing, *Octopussy*. The script—officially by Lorenzo Semple Jr., with ample uncredited additions by British writers Dick Clement and Ian La Frenais—acknowledged Connery and Bond's advancing years (Connery was in his early fifties), and was partly a sequel to the early adventures, partly a tongue-in-cheek homage.

The new M (Edward Fox) isn't impressed with Bond and sends him to Shrublands, a health farm. There, he encounters the sadistic Fatima Blush (Barbara Carrera) and her charge, a USAF pilot, Jack Petachi, whose eye has been changed to duplicate the US president's. This enables SPECTRE to steal two live warheads, which they intend to use to extort a fortune from NATO. Bond is sent to the Bahamas in search of the weapons, and follows Petachi's sister Domino (Kim Basinger), and her lover, Maximilian Largo (Klaus Maria Brandauer), to Nice, France. Bond is captured while investigating Largo's yacht, the *Flying Saucer*, and taken to Largo's base at Palmyra in North Africa. After escaping, and with help from Felix Leiter (Bernie Casey), he locates the bombs beneath the Tears of Allah oasis, and Domino kills Largo before he can detonate one of them.

Many of the traditional Bond trademarks are present and correct—he drinks Absolut vodka—although he's smoking cigars rather than cigarettes now. He's more of a teacher than a doer since the new M arrived, but he slips back into the old 007 ways once the mission begins, confident in his own abilities. (When Largo asks if he loses as gracefully as he wins, Bond replies, "I wouldn't know—I've never lost.") He's respectfully polite to the new M, even if he doesn't agree with his methods; M has little time for him, though, believing that the problems Bond faced at Shrublands were because he was caught seducing someone's wife, and dismissing Bond's (accurate) theory about how SPECTRE got control of the weapon. (Contrast this with the same scene in *Thunderball*, where M backs Bond over others' objections.) He does backtrack after Bond is proved right, however, even offering lunch at his club.

Moneypenny is relieved when Bond is back in business, even if Nigel Small-Fawcett (the British man in the Bahamas, played for laughs by Rowan Atkinson) is concerned, since Bond's reputation has preceded him. He's as charming with women as ever, enjoying the attentions of Nurse Fearing (Prunella Gee) at Shrublands, and pointing out to Fatima Blush that "going down, one should always be relaxed." He has a high tolerance of pain—more than Largo, but only just—and can dance the tango assuredly.

At the end of the mission, though, Bond retires, despite Small-Fawcett telling him that "M says that without you in the service, he fears for the security of the civilized world." Bond won't be drawn, though—"Never again," he vows. As Connery's own website describes it, he is a "much wiser and more mature Bond."

Even more so than *Diamonds Are Forever*, *Never Say Never Again* drew a line under the

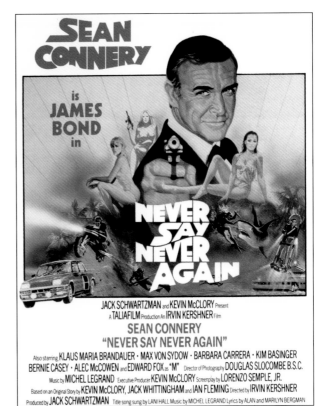

*Michel Landi's artwork for Connery's return in* Never Say Never Again.

Connery era. Both he and his Bond came back to save the world one last time, and from the moment he's revealed through the haze of smoke over the gambling table in *Dr. No* to that final sign-off (and wink to the camera) in *Never Say Never Again*, Connery *was* James Bond to many people, arguably more so than Ian Fleming's original creation. His is still the benchmark against which all versions of Bond are judged, and it is a legacy that has stayed with the actor throughout his career. His Bond is not the character that Fleming created—the sense of humor and the sophistication, particularly in the early films, are markedly different, and the increasingly tetchy relationship with M is a long way from how it's portrayed in the books—but even now, over thirty years since he made his last appearance in the role, it's still Connery that many look to as the archetypal 007.

Sean Connery continued making films for a further twenty years after his return as Bond, and while his final live-action movie, *The League of Extraordinary Gentlemen*, may not have been his finest, he was playing another British literary great: Allan Quatermain—H. Rider Haggard's hero from *King Solomon's Mines*. The nearest he came to reprising Bond? As John Patrick Mason, a British spy and the only man ever to successfully escape from Alcatraz, as seen in *The Rock*—in which Connery proved that he'd never lost his ability to headline an action feature.

# CHAPTER 006

# GEORGE LAZENBY: THE AUSTRALIAN BOND

**W**HEN SEAN CONNERY DECIDED THAT HE HAD HAD ENOUGH OF THE ATTENTION OF THE PRESS DURING THE FILMING OF *YOU ONLY LIVE TWICE* AND REFUSED TO SIGN UP FOR A FURTHER STINT AS OO7, HARRY SALTZMAN AND CUBBY BROCCOLI HAD A NUMBER OF KEY DECISIONS TO MAKE. WAS THE SERIES BIGGER THAN ITS STAR? WOULD AUDIENCES ACCEPT SOMEONE ELSE IN THE ROLE OF JAMES BOND?

The new OO7 was Australian model and actor George Lazenby, who was best known for a commercial in which he carried a giant bar of Fry's chocolate on a beach. He won the role over some stiff competition—*Life* magazine chronicled the process, including photos from the screen tests of the other candidates—with director Peter Hunt believing that he could hone Lazenby's raw talent.

To make the transition easier, the producers surrounded their new actor with a lot of the trappings of the old—the poster, the title sequence, and numerous references

**OPPOSITE:** *The body language is revealing as co-stars George Lazenby and Diana Rigg pose for the cameras.* **RIGHT:** *George Lazenby surrounded by a bevy of Bond beauties on the Piz Gloria set.*

within the film made it abundantly clear that this was still the same James Bond that people had spent the past seven years watching in the cinema. M, Miss Moneypenny, and Q treated him in exactly the same way.

As events transpired, Lazenby and the Bond franchise were not a good fit: some believed Lazenby was unable to handle fame, antagonizing those who had backed him, while he himself felt unsupported by the producers and resigned, becoming a one-film wonder.

## ON HER MAJESTY'S SECRET SERVICE (1969)

In *OHMSS*, Bond is still on the trail of Blofeld (played by Telly Savalas) when he meets Tracy di Vicenzo (Diana Rigg), the unhappy daughter of Unione Corse boss Marc-Ange Draco (Gabriele Ferzetti). He agrees to help Tracy if Draco will assist him in finding Blofeld, which eventually leads 007 to Piz Gloria, a clinic in Switzerland where Blofeld is preparing biological weapons. Bond falls in love with Tracy, but shortly after their marriage she is shot and killed by Blofeld and his partner, Irma Bunt (Ilse Steppat).

*LEFT: An unusual British two-tone version of Frank McCarthy and Robert McGinnis' artwork for* On Her Majesty's Secret Service. *BELOW: Bond and Blofeld come face to face, apparently for the first time, in this lobby card.*

For all that the producers went to the effort to emphasize the similarities, there were some differences between Connery and Lazenby's interpretations of Bond. As we discover from the opening part of the film, this Bond can handle himself very well in a down and dirty fight. He likes Dom Pérignon champagne, and knows his caviar and perfumes. He takes his martini shaken not stirred; smokes, using the same cigarette case first seen in *Dr. No*; and is apparently superstitious about the number thirteen (he throws a knife at a different date on a calendar to avoid it). He keeps souvenirs of some of his past adventures in his office (although, in reality, the items Bond picks up to examine he couldn't possibly have retained), and he has a physically playful relationship with Miss Moneypenny, pinching her backside. He's able to adopt a posh English accent to impersonate Sir Hilary Bray. He has heard of Marc-Ange Draco, head of the Unione Corse, and he is willing to work with someone clearly

ABOVE: *Mr. and Mrs. James Bond prepare to leave for their (short-lived) honeymoon at the end of* On Her Majesty's Secret Service. **RIGHT:** *Yves Thos's portrait of George Lazenby as 007 on the marquee at the London premiere at the Odeon, Leicester Square.*

on the wrong side of the law in order to achieve a higher goal: this is the first time that we see Bond go "rogue," directly disobeying orders from M.

Perhaps most importantly, this is the first time we see Bond fall in love. In previous films, he has been flirtatious, willing to use sex as a weapon for his own ends. However, when he rescues Tracy, something in him reacts to her vulnerability, and, although it seems initially as if he's only with her in order to get help from Draco, as the film progresses, it becomes clear that genuine affection is developing. By the end, he is willing to give up being in the Secret Service for her, knowing that he can't remain an agent and commit fully to her as a married man. The sequence at the race track, where Bond is rescued by Tracy, shows a vulnerability and exhaustion—possibly even fear—in 007 that hadn't been seen previously; the end of the film, as he sits with her still-warm corpse, shows that, despite the cynical trappings, his heart can still be broken. This, of course, brought Lazenby's interpretation—thanks perhaps more to Richard Maibaum's script than the actor's performance—closer to Fleming's character: of all the early movies, this is the one that hews closest to its source material.

Lazenby did reprise the role—unofficially—on at least three occasions: as a mysterious Aston Martin-driving, tuxedoed secret agent who assists Robert Vaughn's Napoleon Solo in the 1983 TV Movie *The Return of the Man From U.N.C.L.E.*; in "Diamonds Aren't Forever," an episode of the new *Alfred Hitchcock Presents*; and in "Help, I've Skyfallen and I Can't Get Up," a sketch from Canadian show *This Hour Has 22 Minutes*.

From Vesper Lynd in the first novel, *Casino Royale*, to Eve Moneypenny in the most recent film, *Skyfall*, James Bond has never been short of female company. Sometimes the ladies involved have been unwilling fellow travelers on Bond's adventures—like Honey Rider in both book and film of *Dr. No*; others have been fellow agents (Anya Amasova in *The Spy Who Loved Me*, or Ariadne Alexandrou in Robert Markham's *Colonel Sun*). Very occasionally, James falls in love with them: Vesper Lynd and (the novel's) Tiffany Case both tempt Bond to resign from the Secret Service. He even marries Tracy di Vicenzo, the daughter of Unione Corse boss Marc-Ange Draco, in *OHMSS*. However, Mr. and Mrs. Bond's happiness is cut short when she is killed by Blofeld and Irma Bunt—not that Bond forgets Tracy: the film Bond lays flowers at her grave in *For Your Eyes Only*, while the literary agent remembers her on multiple occasions in the continuation novels.

"A Bond girl must be a strong and independent woman, but at the same time charming and sensual," *Quantum of Solace*'s Camille, Olga Kurylenko, pointed out. "Those opposite qualities combined together make her interesting. She must be strong but at the same time feminine." Many of the other actresses who have portrayed the women on screen have been adamant that they were breaking the mold, and not just hanging off 007's arm. In fact, that's being unfair to some of the earliest of the Bond heroines: Ursula Andress's Honey Rider was fending for herself when she met Bond and Quarrel on Crab Key Island (Fleming's Honeychile Rider taught herself to read from an encyclopedia); Honor Blackman's Pussy Galore was the head of her own Flying Circus (and her lesbian qualities were explicit in Fleming's text). The characters

**TOP:** Sean Connery and Ursula Andress have fun on the beach in Jamaica during the filming of Dr. No.
**ABOVE:** Roger Moore strikes a typical Bond pose protecting his first leading lady Jane Seymour in this publicity shot from Live and Let Die.

Fleming created often had some perceived flaw—childhood abuse, or a terrible scar—which Bond's innate virility helped them to overcome.

In the films, there were times when the independence the characters showed initially disappeared quite quickly: Tatiana Romanova and Tiffany Case rapidly came to rely on Bond, as did Solitaire (Jane Seymour) in *Live and Let Die*, and Mary Goodnight (Britt Ekland) in *The Man with the Golden Gun* (a shame, as the character originally had been Bond's secretary, and Fleming's version might have improved the movie).

Perhaps coincidentally, after Harry Saltzman ceased to be involved with the 007 films, the strength of the female characters grew, and that has continued with Barbara Broccoli now co-producing the series. On paper (and in Christopher Wood's novel), Major Anya Amasova (Barbara Bach) is Bond's equal, as should be Dr. Holly Goodhead, the CIA agent embedded in Hugo Drax's Moonraker project. Melina Havelock (Carole Bouquet) in *For Your Eyes Only*, and Octopussy herself (Maud Adams) were both stronger characters than some of their forebears; unfortunately, Tanya Roberts's Stacey Sutton in *A View to a Kill* was con-

sistently overshadowed by Grace Jones's May Day, and although Maryam d'Abo's Kara Milovy starts strongly in *The Living Daylights*, she's increasingly a liability to Bond as the film progresses.

Stronger women did assist Bond in the next three films: Lupe Lamora and Pam Bouvier (Talisa Soto and Carey Lowell respectively) in *Licence to Kill*, Natalya Simonova (Izabella Scorupco) in *GoldenEye*, and Chinese intelligence agent Wai Ling (Michelle Yeoh) in *Tomorrow Never Dies* remained independent throughout the films in which they appeared. Denise Richards's Dr. Christmas Jones suffered a similar fate to Stacey Sutton, with Sophie Marceau's Elektra King making far more of an impression in *The World Is Not Enough* as an independent character, even if she was quite definitely not on the side of the angels. The balance was redressed for *Die Another Day*, with Halle Berry's NSA agent Jinx considered such a rounded character that serious plans were drawn for a spin-off centered around her—the first time that such plans progressed beyond vague speculation (as had happened with Michelle Yeoh's Wai Ling a few years earlier), although MGM elected not to follow through with the project.

After Vesper Lynd (Eva Green) nearly breaks his heart in *Casino Royale*, Daniel Craig's Bond was matched with revenge-seeking Camille Montes (Olga Kurylenko) in *Quantum of Solace* (a rare occasion where Bond does not sleep with the heroine; in the books, this happened in *Moonraker*—at the end of the book when he is bent on seducing Gala Brand, he is introduced to her fiancé). *Skyfall* saw the highly independent MI6 agent Eve (Naomie Harris) make her debut, only providing Bond (and the audience) with her surname at the very end of the picture: Moneypenny.

*Eva Green and Daniel Craig at the photocall in Venice during the filming of* Casino Royale.

This fundamentally altered one of the central poles of the Bond franchise: the unresolved sexual tension between M's faithful secretary, Moneypenny, and 007. This is present in the books (in *Thunderball*, we learn that she often dreamed "hopelessly" about Bond), although Fleming did provide 007 with his own secretaries, Loelia Ponsonby and Mary Goodnight. Their flirtatious relationship with Bond was transferred to the movies' Moneypenny, which was then maintained in the continuation novels (although Bond does briefly have a new secretary by the unlikely name of Chastity Vain— you have to suspect that John Gardner wasn't taking things too seriously toward the end of his time).

*Lois Maxwell adopts a rather slinkier pose than Miss Moneypenny would normally approve*

The nature of the Bond/Moneypenny scenes altered depending on the actors involved: Sean Connery, George Lazenby, and Roger Moore interacted with Lois Maxwell, whose Moneypenny clearly yearned to simply be with them (exemplified by her comment about being happy just to receive a tulip in *Diamonds Are Forever*). Timothy Dalton's Bond was opposite a very flirtatious Caroline Bliss, while Pierce Brosnan's Bond enjoyed verbal sparring with Samantha Bond's Moneypenny—who was given some great putdowns. Moneypenny was absent from Daniel Craig's first two films, before the arrival of Eve, a feisty agent responsible for shooting 007 from the top of a train, who shows great loyalty to the new M, Mallory. Whether this Bond and Moneypenny have slept together depends on the audience's interpretation of their comments to each other in the casino.

And, of course, no discussion of the women in Bond's life now can fail to add M herself, as embodied by Judi Dench. Given the name Barbara Mawdsley in Raymond Benson's novels, set concurrent with the Pierce Brosnan era, there are actually at least two alternate versions of this M: the one who appeared with Brosnan's Bond; and the one who promotes Bond to 00 status shortly before *Casino Royale*. The former initially regards Bond as a "sexist, misogynist dinosaur, a relic of the Cold War, whose boyish charms, [are] wasted on me," although the relationship warms. The latter seems to have almost a maternal concern for Bond (something noted by *Quantum of Solace* director Marc Forster), which becomes explicit in *Skyfall*.

There is always great interest in the press when the new Bond heroine is announced—perhaps more so than for the villain's identity—and there will always be plenty of actresses like Morena Baccarin, who will admit that being a "Bond girl" is on their bucket list . . .

# CHAPTER 007

# ROGER MOORE: *THE URBANE BOND*

**T**HERE WAS NEVER ANY DOUBT THAT THE PRODUCERS OF THE 007 SERIES WOULD NEED TO FIND A NEW LEADING MAN AFTER *DIAMONDS ARE FOREVER* FINISHED SHOOTING. SEAN CONNERY HAD MADE HIS POSITION ABUNDANTLY CLEAR, AND IT WAS TIME FOR A FRESH JAMES BOND.

Producers United Artists were in favor of an American 007, with Burt Reynolds, Paul Newman, John Gavin (again), and Robert Redford all under consideration. An approach was made to Clint Eastwood, who refused on the grounds that he believed an Englishman should play the part. Cubby Broccoli agreed, with screen tests given by various actors, including future Sherlock Holmes Jeremy Brett, Simon Oates, and Julian Glover.

In the end, Broccoli and Harry Saltzman turned to Roger Moore, whom they had first met in a gaming house on Curzon Street, London, in the early 1960s, soon after he had begun to play another famous British fictional character: Simon Templar, alias *The Saint*. They had approached Moore about playing 007 when Connery had first indicated his desire to leave after *You Only Live*

**OPPOSITE:** *Roger Moore with a cigarette and glass of wine rather than James Bond's usual cigar and vodka martini.* **ABOVE:** *Looking for a new Bond: Harry Saltzman (left) and Albert "Cubby" Broccoli (right) assess the potential replacement 007s.*

*Twice*, but Moore elected to remain with *The Saint* for one more season when plans for a Cambodia-set Bond film fell through. Although Moore maintains that the producers complained that he was "too fat" and his hair was "too long," contracts were signed and a new Bond was announced to the world.

Roger George Moore was born in Stockwell, London, on October 27, 1927 (making him forty-five, supposedly too old to be in the 00 section, when he began playing the part). After national service and training at the Royal Academy of Dramatic Art (RADA)—where he was classmates with Lois Maxwell, who played Miss Moneypenny in all his Bond films—Moore appeared in various movies and TV shows before being cast as Sir Wilfred of Ivanhoe, the lead character in an adaptation of Sir Walter Scott's romantic novel, and shortly afterwards as Beau Maverick, the English cousin of James Garner's Bret Maverick in the fourth season of the Western series *Maverick*. Soon after that, he was cast as Simon Templar in *The Saint*, a role he played for 118 episodes across seven years. Two movies—*Crossplot* and *The Man Who Haunted Himself*—followed before he became the highest-paid TV actor in the world for the action/adventure series *The Persuaders!*, which teamed him with quirky American actor Tony Curtis. When *The Persuaders!* failed to do sufficiently well in America to warrant a second season, Moore became available for the part of Bond.

Moore has always been self-deprecating about his acting ability—his habit of raising one or other eyebrow has frequently been pilloried by satirists—and it is true to say that some of his own sardonic humor was carried through from Simon Templar to Lord Brett Sinclair (his role in *The Persuaders!*) and into 007. Screenwriter Tom Mankiewicz decided to amend Bond's screen persona to provide a more comfortable fit for Moore, adding more comedy scenes and allowing a more light-hearted approach. Moore himself read through Fleming's books and was inspired by the comment that Bond did not enjoy killing—it was something he had to do, and could do well, but not something from which he derived pleasure.

## *LIVE AND LET DIE* (1973)

In *Live and Let Die*, Bond is sent to New York to investigate the death of an MI6 agent—one of three to have been killed in mysterious circumstances. Their deaths are the work of Caribbean dictator Dr. Kananga (Yaphet Kotto), who uses the persona of crime

lord Mr. Big to run a drug-distribution network through America, and who believes he can see the future through the tarot-reading powers of his virginal assistant, Solitaire (Jane Seymour). Bond meets Big and Solitaire in New York and then, working with CIA agents Felix Leiter (David Hedison) and Rosie Carver (Gloria Hendry)—who is, in fact, a double agent—travels to Kananga's island, San Monique. Bond seduces and rescues Solitaire, taking her to New Orleans, but they are recaptured and Kananga reveals his double identity. Bond is left to be eaten by crocodiles but escapes, returning to San Monique to save Solitaire from death in a voodoo ritual, before killing Kananga. Bond has to dispose of Kananga's henchman Tee Hee (Julius Harris) before he and Solitaire can continue her lessons in love . . .

While George Lazenby's Bond was clearly cut from the same cloth as Connery's, Moore's interpretation of the role was very different, as epitomized by the scene midway through *Live and Let Die* where, suspended dozens of feet in the air on

a hang-glider, waiting to swoop into the villain's lair, he's nonchalantly puffing away on a huge cigar. The first time we meet him, he's in bed with a young Italian agent, Miss Caruso. Miss Moneypenny assists Bond in keeping her hidden from M's disapproving eyes when, very unusually, the head of the Secret Service comes to Bond's luxury apartment, in which there are many modern conveniences for the time, including a cappuccino machine. This Bond enjoys a luxurious existence—he has his boots made for him (as did Baines, one of the murdered MI6 agents), and orders a bottle of Bollinger champagne for himself and his unexpected bride (aka Rosie Carver). M seems almost contemptuous of such luxuries.

Unusually, but perhaps in a futile attempt to blend into his surroundings as a white man in the black-dominated Harlem district, he orders a Bourbon and water rather than a vodka martini, but, being Bond, he has to have it in a specific way—without ice (which would have cost extra anyway!). He's as nonchalant in the face of danger as ever, telling Solitaire to "stay right there" since he won't be long, even as he's being taken out to be "wasted." His idea of killing time is to help Carver with her training—or, as he tells her, "lick you into shape"—although she initially decides that she wants a separate bedroom (she doesn't stay there long). He's as chauvinistic as ever (Carver's "compensations speak for themselves"), and puts off interrogating Carver about her treachery until after they've slept together one more time. He seduces Solitaire by rigging the deck of tarot cards so she believes it is fated that they will be lovers (although he does admit it, slightly shamefacedly, later when he realizes how upset Solitaire is by the loss of her virginity), and is happy to assist with her education, rather than "go off half-cocked"—a rather irresponsible attitude given that time is against them. He also teaches her how to play gin rummy.

His fighting prowess is undiminished, dealing with assorted thugs and hoodlums along the way, killing them when required, and he can swim considerable distances. He is quick to make use of whatever comes to hand—using his shaving-foam dispenser and cigar to create a crude flamethrower—and can drive pretty much anything from an old London double-decker bus (although he is rather careless about checking the height of the bridges he passes beneath), to a speedboat.

**ABOVE:** *Roger Moore keeps a firm grip on his star chair at the airport location.*
**LEFT:** *Meeting royalty at the London premiere: Roger Moore and Jane Seymour joke with Princess Anne.*

# THE MAN WITH THE GOLDEN GUN (1974)

Many of these qualities are reprised in Roger Moore's second outing as 007, which followed in 1974. *The Man with the Golden Gun* is one of the less well-regarded Bond movies, perhaps because it tried too hard to cash in on the trend for kung-fu films prevalent in cinema at the time (an attempt to pursue the sci-fi audience a few years later with *Moonraker* was similarly poorly regarded by fans). The scene in the training school, where Bond is pushed aside by two school girls who then put a host of fighters out of action, is embarrassing and out of place in a Bond film.

Bond is put on leave after Francisco Scaramanga (Christopher Lee)—the so-called Man with the Golden Gun, a highly paid assassin based on an island in Red Chinese waters—apparently indicates that 007 is his next target. Bond has previously been searching for a missing scientist, as well as the Solex, a key component of a solar-energy project, which he discovers that Scaramanga has obtained. The trail leads to the Far East, where Scaramanga's mistress, Miss Anders (Maud Adams), agrees to bring Bond the Solex if he will kill Scaramanga for her—007 is the one man her lover fears, which is why she sent a bullet with his number on it to the Secret Service. However, Scaramanga kills Miss Anders, and flies back to his island, with Bond's assistant, Mary Goodnight (Britt Ekland), inadvertently aboard his flying car. Bond follows and, after a duel between the men, kills Scaramanga and retrieves the Solex.

The slightly sour relationship between Bond and M, which began in *Diamonds Are Forever*, continues here—M has no problem thinking of people who would want to kill 007. "Jealous husbands, outraged chefs, humiliated tailors. The list

*Tom Jung's less well-known poster for Roger Moore's* The Man with the Golden Gun *was nicknamed the "Villain."*

Co-stars from three eras of Bond: Goldfinger's *Honor Blackman (left)*, The Man with the Golden Gun's *Christopher Lee (middle)* and On Her Majesty's Secret Service's *Diana Rigg in January 1974*.

is endless," he points out. He's not at all pleased with Bond when he disrupts another operation in Hong Kong: "I almost wish that Scaramanga had a contract on you," he barks. In fact, M is in an impatient mood for much of the film, snapping at Q on more than one occasion, and despairing, "Of all the fouled-up, half-witted operations!"

The flirting with Moneypenny is in full force—although, for once, she is spiky when Bond tries to wheedle information from her—and Bond is at his charming best when trying to get a bullet used to kill a fellow OO agent from a cabaret dancer. He and Goodnight have some form of romantic history prior to her posting to Hong Kong two years earlier; it's not stated that she was the OO section secretary, as she was in the book. She is used to his ways, turning down his seduction initially—"killing a few hours as one of your passing fancies isn't quite my scene"—although she quickly changes her mind (and doesn't object when he tells her "your turn will come"!). Bond performs at his best with Miss Anders to persuade her to betray Scaramanga.

Bond is full of useful information: he has a good working knowledge of KGB-trained assassins, and can match particular bullet calibers to the relevant guns. He can quickly deduce how the process works in Scaramanga's electrical plant on the island, allowing him to instruct Goodnight in its use. When he's allowed to, he can hold his own in a fight against multiple opponents, and he has "never killed a midget before." He can be ruthless when necessary, aiming a gun at the groin of a potential informant and warning him to speak "or forever hold your piece," and twisting Miss Anders' arm behind her back painfully as well as slapping her. When driving, he can quickly assess the most unlikely options, such as the use of a rickety broken bridge as a ramp. He seems surprised that Hai Fat hasn't heard of him—in fact, he seems to revel in the fact that "there are very few people who haven't heard of Bond," which misses the point of the word "secret" in his job description!

He prefers the 1962 Dom Pérignon to the 1964, and still smokes cigars. His sartorial elegance is rather muted, wearing a checked sport jacket when he arrives on Scaramanga's island—and he can change clothes remarkably quickly, adopting the suit worn by Scaramanga's mannequin of him as a disguise. He has a quip for many occasions, although he won't trade words with Scaramanga, pointing out that there's "a useful four-letter word and you're full of it." He denies gaining pleasure from most kills—specifically excepting Scaramanga from that list—and claims "those I kill are themselves killers."

## THE SPY WHO LOVED ME (1977)

The partnership between Cubby Broccoli and Harry Saltzman had not been harmonious for some years, with the pair dividing responsibility for the films between them rather than working together (*Live and Let Die* was controlled by Saltzman; *Golden Gun* by Broccoli). Certain decisions, such as casting, were joint, but the day-to-day control was ceded to one or other. Unlike Broccoli, Saltzman was also involved with other film projects, none of which really took off in the way the 007 franchise had; there were agreements between the pair to wind up Danjaq S.A., the Swiss company in which the rights were invested, but these weren't followed through. Saltzman also had personal difficulties, with his wife suffering from terminal cancer, and shortly after *The Man with the Golden Gun* premiered, he sold his half-share in the franchise to United Artists.

Broccoli knew that his first solo Bond film, released in 1977, would need to be something spectacular. There were only two Bond novels left that hadn't been filmed: *Moonraker* and *The Spy Who Loved Me*. Ian Fleming had instructed that only

**LEFT:** *With an unprecedented three years between films, audiences had to be reminded of the scale of the franchise in Bob Peak's stylized poster.* **ABOVE:** *The train fight with Jaws, and Bond speeding on a jetbike to save Anya, are some of the classic action sequences in the film.*

the title of the latter could be sold to EON; as discussed on page 29, the book was an experiment in presenting Bond differently, which hadn't attracted the success Fleming had hoped for. The *Daily Express* comic strip had incorporated the events of the novel into a larger story, but EON had to start from scratch—although the steel-capped teeth of hoodlum Sol Horror were referenced in the movie's henchman Jaws.

After numerous different storylines were discussed—and some reluctantly discarded, since they featured Ernst Stavro Blofeld and SPECTRE, elements which were the subject of court proceedings by Kevin McClory—the eventual script by Richard Maibaum and Christopher Wood effectively recycled the plot of the movie *You Only Live Twice*, with submarines replacing space capsules.

*Curt Jurgens at the UK premiere of* The Spy Who Loved Me *on July 7, 1977.*

When British and Soviet nuclear submarines mysteriously disappear, James Bond and Russian agent Triple X, Major Anya Amasova (Barbara Bach), are sent by their respective governments to investigate. The trail leads to Egypt, where the pair are forced to call a truce as they encounter the steel-toothed giant Jaws (Richard Kiel), and are then instructed to team up to deal with shipping magnate and scientist Karl Stromberg (Curt Jurgens). Using Bond's specially equipped Lotus they check out Stromberg's underwater base, the *Atlantis*, and start to become close—until Anya is informed that Bond was responsible for the death of her lover. She tells him that, once the mission is over, she will kill him. While on an American submarine, 007 and Anya are captured by Stromberg: his new supertanker, the *Liparus*, contains the hijacked submarines. Bond aids the various submariners to escape and prevents Stromberg from starting a nuclear war. Bond then rescues Anya from *Atlantis*, killing Stromberg in the process, and she decides not to follow through with her threat.

Director Lewis Gilbert wanted to move Moore's portrayal of Bond away from Sean Connery's version, and he helped to create the smoother, more urbane 007 with which Moore is best associated. This Bond is definitely supposed to be the same person as the man played by Connery and Lazenby, though—Anya makes reference to his ill-fated marriage to Tracy, and Bond admits that he's "sensitive" on the subject. We also learn that he attended Cambridge University alongside the future Sheikh Hosein, and was assigned to HMS *Ark Royal* during his time in the Royal Navy—for the second time in the series, we see him in his full naval uniform. He claims that he has never failed on a mission.

Although he's respectful of Anya's position as his counterpart in the KGB, and knows enough about her to be able to order a drink for her, he can be very patronizing toward her—notably when she is trying to get the truck into gear as they attempt to escape from Jaws. He's cold-blooded about the job they both do, perhaps more so than he's been previously, reminding her that he was in a kill or be killed situation when he was being shot at by her fiancé in the Alps. He is ruthless when on the quest for information—he holds Sandor, a henchman, over the side of a building, gets what he wants, and then lets him fall to his death—and when dealing with Stromberg, firing his gun four times.

His prowess with the ladies continues: he stays the night with his old university friend and enjoys the female delights on offer, and eventually persuades Anya Amasova into his arms (keeping the British end up in doing so). He is prepared to be distracted to a certain extent by Fekkesh's woman, Felicca, but when it's clear she's setting him up, he has no hesitation in spinning her round so she receives the bullet meant for him. He flirts with Stromberg's pilot Naomi (Caroline Munro) but has no regrets about blowing her up after she tries to kill him and Anya.

Bond continues to be flippant in the face of danger—there are various quips about Egyptian builders, or feather-covered motorcyclists who still can't fly—and can hold his own in a fistfight. His wide-ranging knowledge now encompasses defusing a nuclear bomb (although he's never actually had to do it before), as well as varieties of tropical fish, and he likes the 1952 Dom Pérignon. He expects Max Kalba to know who he is—and is a little put out that Kalba is unimpressed.

*Barbara Bach and Roger Moore share a joke as they pose with the Lotus Espirit to promote* The Spy Who Loved Me.

# MOONRAKER *(1979)*

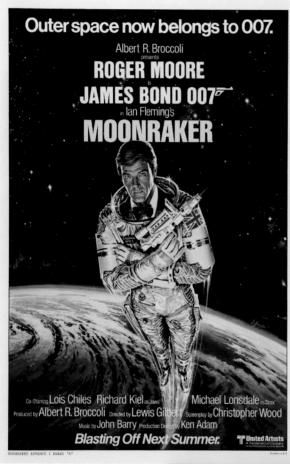

Although the end credits of *The Spy Who Loved Me* indicated that *For Your Eyes Only* would follow, the next film, released in 1979, was *Moonraker*, designed to cash in on the craze for sci-fi films that appeared in the wake of George Lucas's *Star Wars* in 1977. With one of the same writers (Christopher Wood) and director (Lewis Gilbert) as *The Spy Who Loved Me*, the portrayal of 007 didn't alter much.

When a Moonraker shuttle belonging to billionaire Hugo Drax (Michael Lonsdale) is stolen from the back of an RAF jet in flight, 007 is sent to Drax's plant in California to investigate. He becomes suspicious after attempts on his life and breaks into Drax's safe, finding blueprints for glassware. He keeps crossing paths with Dr. Holly Good-head (Lois Chiles), a CIA agent embedded

***ABOVE:*** *Trying to take on Star Wars at its own game: Dan Goozee's teaser poster for Moonraker emphasizes the sci-fi elements of the film.* ***RIGHT:*** *Richard Kiel listens as Michael Lonsdale charms the Duke of Edinburgh at the Royal Premiere of Moonraker in June 1979.* ***OPPOSITE:*** *Bernard Lee and his wife at the premiere of Moonraker, the last Bond film in which he would appear.*

with Drax, and discovers that a deadly toxin is being placed inside glass globes. The trail leads them to Brazil, where Holly is captured; the toxin comes from an Amazonian flower, and in the heart of the jungle Bond finds Drax's headquarters. He and Holly hijack *Moonraker 6* and travel to Drax's orbiting space station, from where Drax intends to destroy life on Earth and start afresh with genetically pure humans. With the help of Jaws, who has been working for Drax but realizes that there's no place for him in the new order, Bond and Holly destroy the space station and the toxin-filled globes.

Bond is physically fitter than most, able to endure higher g-forces than the normal man, which comes in handy when he journeys into "outer space" in the Moonraker. His reputation precedes him, probably including the part about being a chauvinistic ladies' man (his reaction to Dr. Goodhead being a woman is not his finest hour): he seduces Drax's assistant Corinne (Corinne Clery), and Holly, as well as Brazilian MI6 agent Manuela (Emily Bolton). He's still quick with a joke in difficult situations, and seems to have extreme difficulty with the concept of being a "secret" agent, driving a "hover-gondola" around St. Mark's Square in Venice to the disbelief of the crowds.

The acerbic relationship with M has gone—he trusts 007 to rectify the difficult situation with Drax quickly. Bond's scientific knowledge extends to being able to identify the chemical composition of a plant; he knows around which river black orchids grow, and their particular effects.

## *FOR YOUR EYES ONLY* (1981)

Everyone involved with the 007 series realized that, after the excesses of *Moonraker*, they would need to restore Bond's credibility with the next film, and 1981's *For Your Eyes Only*—which combined the revenge element from the short story of that name and the drug-smuggling plot of "Risico"—saw a much more serious Bond. This was the first film directed by John Glen, who would helm the movies throughout the 1980s. Elaborate bases for the villain were out; Citroën 2CV cars rather than gadget-filled Lotus Esprits were in.

After a British spy ship is sunk in the Ionian Sea, the race is on to retrieve the ATAC, a key communications system, from the wreckage. Marine archaeologist Sir

**LEFT:** *Brian Bysoth's controversial painting for the first Bond film of the 1980s was based on a design by Eric Pulford (in some countries, the bikini bottom was considerably enlarged).* **BELOW:** *Bond (Roger Moore) is captured after the murder of Countess Lisl;* **BOTTOM:** *Bond snuggling up with Melina Havelock.*

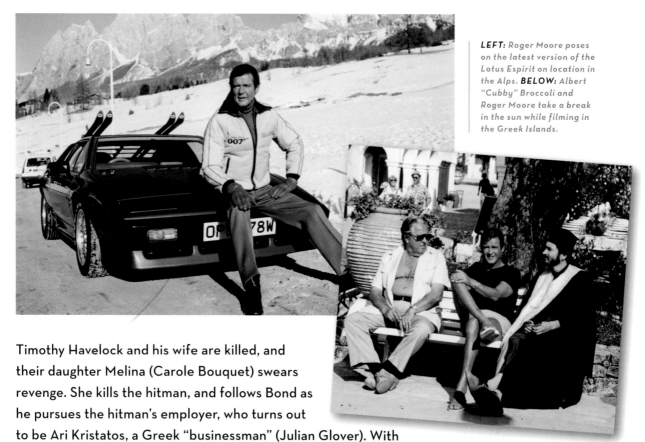

Timothy Havelock and his wife are killed, and their daughter Melina (Carole Bouquet) swears revenge. She kills the hitman, and follows Bond as he pursues the hitman's employer, who turns out to be Ari Kristatos, a Greek "businessman" (Julian Glover). With help from Kristatos's rival, Milos Columbo (Topol), Bond discovers that Kristatos sank the ship deliberately. Bond and Melina retrieve the ATAC from the wreck, but are captured by Kristatos's men. They are able to follow Kristatos to an abandoned mountaintop monastery, where the Greek plans to hand the ATAC to KGB General Gogol (Walter Gotell). Columbo kills Kristatos after Bond prevents Melina from doing so; 007 destroys the ATAC to stop Gogol getting it.

The film opens with Bond placing flowers on his wife's grave (her date of death is given as 1969), before he turns the tables on an old nemesis (Blofeld, although it's never stated as such for legal reasons). He counsels Melina against going out for revenge—which is a little odd, given what he's just done to the man who killed his wife. He's a little hypocritical in that respect: he also kicks a car off the edge of a cliff with the murderer of a fellow MI6 agent inside. Although he's still charming, he doesn't try to bed every female he meets. Bibi Dahl (Lynn-Holly Johnson) is too young for him, and Melina only falls into his arms once she has completed his mission. He does,

however, succumb to the ersatz countess Lisl (Cassandra Harris), knowing that she works for Columbo and he can pump her for information.

He can fly a helicopter, although he has some problems with the iconoclastic design of the stick shift on a Citroën 2CV car. He speaks Spanish. His prowess on snow covers many disciplines, not just skiing, and he is a good mountaineer. M is on leave (in reality, actor Bernard Lee died during production and was not recast for this film) and Tanner, the Chief of Staff (James Villiers), doesn't have a lot of time for him (unlike their friendship in Fleming's books). There are a few quips, but overall this is the most subdued and serious Bond for many years.

# OCTOPUSSY (1983)

1983 saw two rival Bonds in theaters at the same time. Connery's return in *Never Say Never Again* made a plot point of the actor's age. Moore's Bond in *Octopussy* never hinted that he was anything other than at the peak of his physical form, and although the film was very serious much of the time, there were some overtly humorous moments that came at the cost of the character.

After 009 dies while bringing a fake Fabergé egg over the Berlin Wall, MI6 try to discover who is selling the real egg; this puts 007 on the trail of exiled Afghani prince Kamal Khan (Louis Jourdan), who is working with Octopussy (Maud Adams), the leader of the Octopus cult. Soviet General Orlov (Steven Berkoff) has been supplying Khan with real treasures and replacing them with fakes; Octopussy's circus has been the cover for the smuggling route from East to West. However, Orlov secretly plans to use a nuclear weapon, which he has hidden within the jewels he is smuggling, to force the Americans to unilaterally disarm after it explodes in West Berlin. Bond uncovers the plan and prevents the bomb from detonating, before he and Octopussy, who is furious at being betrayed, pursue Khan.

Bond is as charming as ever, trying to flatter Miss Moneypenny, while obviously interested in her new (younger) assistant, Miss Penelope Smallbone (Michaela Clavell). He is respectful to M (now played by Robert Brown). He happily goes along with his seduction by Octopussy and Kamal Khan's assistant Magda (Kristina Wayborn). He's good at sleight of hand—he is able to switch the genuine Fabergé egg for the fake without anyone noticing. He thinks a piece that MI6 agent Vijay (Vijay Amritraj) is playing is a "charming" tune (it's the "James Bond Theme"), and he can play backgammon. His capabilities with a nuclear bomb are constantly improving: he took the detonator out of the one on the *Liparus*; in the circus in Berlin, he defuses it completely.

He is politically incorrect, suggesting that money will keep an Indian agent "in curry for a few weeks." He can behave like an adolescent when given the

**TOP:** *Dan Goozee's dynamic artwork for 1983's* Octopussy *puts the Acrostar jet front and center—even if it only makes a brief pre-credits appearance.*
**ABOVE:** *Roger Moore and Maud Adams photographed on the* Octopussy *set.*

chance to play with Q's gadgets—or, indeed, when he has to swing through the trees and can't resist the temptation to issue a Tarzan yell. He's watched—or at least is aware of—British dog trainer Barbara Woodhouse's methods, telling a tiger to "sit" in a particular tone of voice.

Some years earlier, he gave Major Dexter Smythe, Octopussy's father, the opportunity to put his affairs in order when he was sent to arrest him; Smythe committed suicide. He's an honorable man himself, and is not willing to go into business with Octopussy.

## A VIEW TO A KILL (1985)

There's no question that Roger Moore was lacking credibility as 007 in his final film *A View to a Kill*; he was aged fifty-eight when the movie was released in 1985, and the difference between the stuntmen playing Bond and his own inserts was noticeable. For the first time since *The Spy Who Loved Me*, the film had a completely original story, with only Fleming's title and the characters of Bond and M retained from the short story.

Bond recovers a microchip from Siberia, which was designed to withstand an electromagnetic pulse, like those created by Zorin Industries. Max Zorin (Christopher Walken) is a former KGB agent who has gone rogue and plans to flood Silicon Valley to give himself a monopoly over microchip manufacture. With help from geologist Stacey Sutton (Tanya Roberts) and KGB agent Pola Ivanova (Fiona Fullerton), Bond locates Zorin's headquarters and manages to prevent him from exploding devices along the San Andreas and Hayward

Faults, with some help from Zorin's assistant, May Day (Grace Jones), after Zorin abandons her. After Zorin kidnaps Stacey on his airship, Bond grabs the ropes and successfully rescues her, sending Zorin falling to his death.

Bond's wine knowledge is on display again, as he chooses expensive bottles of Bollinger and Lafite Rothschild; when drinking vodka, he prefers Stolichnaya. He's a good cook who can rustle up a good meal quickly. He's also an accomplished horse rider, able to deal with an animal whose adrenalin has been artificially spiked, and he knows how to drive a fire truck. He is awarded the Order of Lenin at the end of the film—the first Westerner to receive it, according to General Gogol.

Unfortunately, he uses some very obvious double entendres throughout the film, although this doesn't seem to prevent various ladies falling into bed (or a mini-submarine) with him.

By the end, Roger Moore's Bond had strayed some considerable distance from Ian Fleming's template, and indeed from Sean Connery's and George Lazenby's portrayal, but for generations of fans he was the definitive 007. Unlike Fleming's spy, or the earlier movie incarnations, there was no question that far too many people knew who James Bond was—as well as his taste in clothes, food, and women—for him to have any chance of succeeding as a secret agent. Quicker with a flippant line than with his Walther PPK, Roger Moore's Bond became the almost-characterless centerpiece in totally incredible blockbusters—none of which prevented the movies from taking good box office, and providing great entertainment.

Moore had talked about stepping down before each of the movies made in the 1980s, but after *A View to a Kill*, it was clear that the time had come for a change. The 007 who followed tried to return the character to his roots.

*OPPOSITE: The very unusual teaser poster for A View to a Kill was designed by Vic Fair and painted by Brian Bysoth; however, EON decided not to use it in the main design by Dan Goozee. Right **TOP**: Singer Grace Jones branched out into acting for Roger Moore's swansong as Bond, pictured here in character as May Day at the press call. **ABOVE**: Christopher Walken as Max Zorin pictured on set.*

# REBOOTING BOND

## *007*

In 2006, audiences around the world were startled to see a very different take on the James Bond they had come to know over twenty films and forty-five years. Although perhaps it wasn't totally credible, the intention was that the agent played by Sean Connery (in his official appearances anyway), George Lazenby, Roger Moore, Timothy Dalton, and Pierce Brosnan was the same man. But with the arrival of Daniel Craig, it wasn't just a new chapter in the 007 story that was beginning: it was a whole new tale. Craig's Bond had never battled SPECTRE; he hadn't been married and widowed thanks to the machinations of Ernst Stavro Blofeld. It was a trick that had been successfully pulled off by the makers of the *Batman* franchise, and it paid off for EON Productions.

However, this wasn't the first time that the producers had considered restarting the Bond saga from scratch or incorporating the change of

actor into the films' narrative. When Sean Connery stepped down after *You Only Live Twice*, the sequel, *OHMSS*, could have begun with Bond undergoing plastic surgery so that Blofeld didn't recognize him (a variant of this was used for the start of *Diamonds Are Forever*). In the end, some cute references—such as the line "This never happened to the other fellow" in the pre-credits scene—were used.

When they knew that the film following *A View to a Kill* would introduce Roger Moore's replacement as Bond, writers Richard Maibaum and Michael G. Wilson penned a treatment (a detailed outline of the story) that showed how James Bond came to enter the Secret Service and acquired his license to kill. The young naval officer would be seen working alongside veteran agent Burton Trevor in a complex tale of drug smuggling, and eventually inherit Trevor's number in the 00 section.

The project needed Cubby Broccoli's blessing before it could be worked up into a full script. It didn't get it. As Maibaum told the *New York Times*, "Mr. Broccoli, who has an uncanny appreciation of what audiences want, among his other great talents, liked it; but he said the audience wasn't interested in Bond as an amateur—as a man learning his trade." The writers were sent back to Ian Fleming's books to seek inspiration, finding it in the short story "The Living Daylights." The movie Bond would eventually be rebooted nearly two decades later.

While such a move on the big screen isn't unusual—the past couple of decades have seen multiple "origin" movies for characters— for it to happen in books is less common. However, that's what Ian Fleming Publications agreed to al-

*Producer Cubby Broccoli on the set of* A View to a Kill. *Knowing precisely what audiences wanted from Bond films, he vetoed a reboot for* The Living Daylights.

low when they commissioned respected American thriller writer Jeffery Deaver to contribute a new entry to the Bond canon for publication in 2011.

The book 007 had been consistently carrying out missions from 1953 to 2003—the same man who encountered Le Chiffre in *Casino Royale* battled *The Man with the Red Tattoo*. Charlie Higson, Samantha Weinberg, and Sebastian Faulks's additions to the saga were all set in that character's past. Deaver, however, was determined to bring Bond into the twenty-first century. "When the Fleming Estate contacted me, I said that I would only want to do it if it were set in the present day," he told the HMSS weblog, "and they said, 'We agree, that is what we were hoping for too.' And the reason for that is the original books were not period pieces, of course. They were a product of their time."

It wasn't just 007 that Deaver updated. His novel features all the familiar faces—Admiral Sir Miles Messervy, Bill Tanner, Felix Leiter, and even Bond's secretary Mary Goodnight are there to assist the agent. The trappings of the Secret Service were brought into the twenty-first century, with Bond using appropriate apps on his smartphone. Unfortunately, despite many positive reviews, this version of the Bond franchise hasn't as yet been revisited.

*Author Jeffery Deaver, who brought the literary Bond firmly into the twenty-first century with his novel Carte Blanche.*

# CHAPTER 008

# TIMOTHY DALTON: THE BLEEDING BOND

ROGER MOORE HAD BEEN CONTRACTED FOR THREE FILMS AS 007, AND BEFORE HE SIGNED UP FOR EACH OF HIS SUBSEQUENT FOUR, THERE WAS A PERIOD WHEN EON WERE NOT CERTAIN IF HE WOULD BE PLAYING THE ROLE AGAIN. DURING THOSE TIMES, OTHER ACTORS WERE CONSIDERED—AND EVEN, IN THE CASE OF JAMES BROLIN FOR OC*TOPUSSY*, SCREEN TESTED FOR THE PART. HOWEVER, AFTER *A VIEW TO A KILL* THERE WAS NO QUESTION OF MOORE RETURNING, AND FROM THE START OF 1986, MANY ACTORS OF THE RIGHT AGE WERE CONSIDERED FOR THE ROLE, INCLUDING MARK GREENSTREET AND TREVOR EVE.

Sam Neill, who had starred as early twentieth-century double-agent Sidney Reilly on television as well as the Antichrist Damien Thorn on the big screen, was the preference of co-producer Michael G. Wilson, director John Glen, and both Dana Broccoli and her daughter Barbara, but Cubby was not so impressed. One of Roger Moore's eventual successors as Simon Templar, Australian Andrew Clarke, was also considered, but he backed out of the casting process when terms couldn't be agreed. His fellow Australian Mel Gibson had been approached by Broccoli in 1982, and United Artists were keen on him now, but the *Mad Max* and *Lethal Weapon* star would only commit to one movie.

**TOP:** John Glen, director of all the Bond films during the 1980s, at the premiere of The Living Daylights. **ABOVE:** The 007 Stage at Pinewood in 1987: the second of the three buildings bearing this name, it burned down in 2006.

Another actor who had been considered in 1982 came to the fore once more now: Pierce Brosnan, the star of comedy detective series *Remington Steele*. When NBC cancelled the show, it seemed his time had come as Bond, but the increased publicity around Brosnan prompted the network to order more episodes, and after they insisted on a full twenty-two-episode season, Cubby Broccoli made it clear that "Remington Steele will not be James Bond." Brosnan's time would come, however.

Focus therefore turned to one of the people who had been on EON's radar for a number of years—theatrical actor Timothy Dalton. There had been vague discussions with him back in 1968 after Connery's first departure, and a meeting in 1980 before *For Your Eyes Only*, but now Dalton was willing to screen test (using scenes from *OHMSS*) and was quickly signed up.

Timothy Peter Dalton was born in Colwyn Bay, North Wales, and was bitten by the acting bug after seeing a production of *Macbeth* when he was sixteen years old. He trained for a time at RADA and toured with the National Youth Theatre, but left RADA because of the "oppressive teachers." His big break in film came in 1968 with *The Lion in Winter*, and he played a memorable Heathcliff in the 1970 movie version of *Wuthering Heights*. He worked on both sides of the Atlantic in both film and television, appearing in the camp classic *Flash Gordon* in 1980 and as Mr. Rochester in the BBC's *Jane Eyre* three years later. He continued to act on stage, and shortly before his casting as 007 was in productions of Shakespeare's *The Taming of the Shrew* and *Antony and Cleopatra*.

Dalton's approach to the part was simple. "In order for the audience to be swept along in this fantasy, you've got to believe in the person," he said in an interview promoting his second film, *Licence to Kill*. "What I'm trying to do is get [Bond] back to being a real person that we can identify with, to show some of his flaws, to show his strengths too." He was frequently seen on set reading and re-reading the original Ian Fleming stories, and in multiple interviews during his time as 007, he referred back to the characterization of Bond as a man on the edge, someone who is close to burn-out and needs chemical assistance—whether it's "uppers," "downers," or just alcohol—to cope with what he has to do.

## *THE LIVING DAYLIGHTS* (1987)

Work on the script for *The Living Daylights* began after Moore had left the part, but before the screenwriters knew who would be his successor. After time spent preparing a story that told Bond's first mission (see 007 Rebooted sidebar on pages 124-5), they devised a tale about smuggling that involved the Russian mission in Afghanistan, using Ian Fleming's short story "The Living Daylights" as the springboard for a new plot.

KGB General Georgi Koskov (Jeroen Krabbé) defects to the West with news that an old operation, Smiet Spionem (SMERSH), has been reactivated; 007 prevents a female sniper from shooting him during his defection. Koskov claims that General Leonid Pushkin (John Rhys-Davies) is in charge of SMERSH, and two 00 agents have already died; he is then abducted from the MI6 safe house. Bond has his doubts about Koskov and Pushkin, so tracks down the sniper, a cellist named Kara Milovy (Maryam d'Abo), who is Koskov's

*The photographic teaser poster for Timothy Dalton's debut. The model's dress was made less translucent in some countries, notably Italy.*

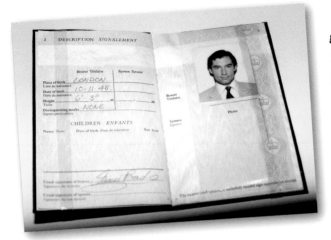

girlfriend. The entire defection was a fake. Bond travels with Kara to Tangiers, where he discovers from Pushkin that Koskov is wanted for embezzlement. Koskov is selling weapons to arms dealer Brad Whitaker (Joe Don Baker), and captures 007. Bond and Kara are taken to Afghanistan, where Koskov is buying opium from the Mujahideen that will then be sold to buy weapons to use against them. Bond allies with the Afghan rebels, led by Kamran Shah (Art Malik), to destroy the opium, then returns to Tangiers to kill Whitaker. Koskov is arrested by Pushkin and returned to Moscow to face trial.

Bond's luck, physical prowess, and charm are all on display in the first few minutes of *The Living Daylights*. He's the third and final target of the SMERSH hit man, so is aware of the potential problem; he clings to the top of a Land Rover which is being driven at manic speeds down the narrow roads of Gibraltar; and then is happy to indulge in an hour—or two—of winding down after the mission with a beautiful woman.

His ways with women are renowned throughout the Service—Saunders, Head of Section V, Vienna, chides him for looking at a beautiful girl rather than focusing

*ABOVE: James Bond's passport as seen in The Living Daylights, giving his date of birth as November 10, 1948.*
*RIGHT: Storyboard designs for the scene at the airfield, drawn before Maryam d'Abo had been cast.*

on the task at hand. He continues to flirt with Moneypenny (now played by Caroline Bliss), although he doesn't seem tempted to take her up on her offer of listening to her Barry Manilow collection at her apartment. However, he seems to fall for Kara, although he has to lie to her that he is a friend of Koskov's in order to gain her trust, and he reluctantly gives in to her demand to bring her cello (although he's grateful for it later). He even defies orders to go on an assignment abroad so he doesn't miss her first concert in the West. He has a friendly, bantering relationship with Q, and is pleased to see Felix Leiter (John Terry). He's pleasant to Koskov to begin with, but when the Russian reveals his scheme, Bond uses a familiar expression: "We have an old saying, too, Georgi—and you're full of it!"

*Timothy Dalton, Maryam d'Abo, and 007's latest Aston Martin at the press call in Vienna to launch* The Living Daylights.

He still has a taste for the finer things in life—he gets a better brand of champagne from Harrods for Koskov because the one on the list "was questionable." He's well known at the hotel in Vienna that he takes Kara to—usually he doesn't require a second bedroom—and they are aware of his drinks requirements. He seems to know the people who operate the Ferris wheel well enough to arrange to be stranded at the top (this could just be a joke, although the timing is very convenient). And he knows a "great restaurant in Karachi." He's back to smoking cigarettes, after the cigars of the Moore years.

Bond is not an indiscriminate killing machine: when he realizes that Kara is an amateur—she "didn't know one end of a rifle from the other"—he simply shoots to scare the living daylights out of her. He will only kill professionals, and if that means M (still played by Robert Brown) fires him for disobeying orders, "I'll thank him for it." He will challenge M when he feels he needs to, particularly when he justifies his instincts, but he refuses the offer of two weeks' leave so that someone else can kill Pushkin: "If it has to be done, I'd rather do it." Pushkin respects him as a fellow professional, who does not kill without reason, and the Russian is pleased that Bond is a good shot (as he proves on numerous occasions with various weapons).

Bond is not the fount of all knowledge that he's been in the past: he is unaware that Stradivarius instruments all have names. Nor is he as quick with a quip when in danger. He can ride a horse, and pilot a plane.

## LICENCE TO KILL

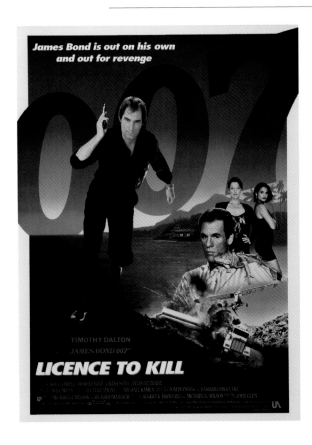

James Bond is out on his own
and out for revenge

TIMOTHY DALTON
JAMES BOND 007

**LICENCE TO KILL**

The success of *The Living Daylights*, with its harder-edged Bond and less of an emphasis on humor, meant that the script of *Licence to Kill* (or *Licence Revoked*, as it was known until market research indicated that many Americans didn't know what "revoked" meant) was tailored to this approach from the start. The story incorporated elements of Fleming's *Live and Let Die* and the short story "The Hildebrand Rarity" into a tale that was "torn straight from the headlines of today's newspapers," according to the film's press release.

Bond is attending the wedding of Della and Felix Leiter (the latter played once more by David Hedison), when the latter is summoned to help capture drug baron Franz Sanchez (Robert Davi). After Sanchez escapes, he takes revenge on the Leiters, killing Della and mutilating Felix; Bond swears vengeance, and despite clear in-structions from M to the contrary, takes off after Sanchez. With the help of former CIA agent Pam Bouvier (Carey Lowell), he inveigles his way into Sanchez's inner circle in the Republic of Isthmus, claiming to be looking for work. He's taken to Sanchez's base, where he is nearly fed into a shredder. Escaping this with Pam's help, he pursues Sanchez, even-tually setting fire to him.

Bond is a driven man throughout this film—the treatment meted out to Felix and Della the catalyst

SENTINEL / WAVEKREST / MANTA SEQUENCES

REVISED 16 JUNE '88 SHEET 1

**ABOVE LEFT:** *In case anyone didn't recognize Dalton, the numbers "007" were plastered across this poster, which artist Brian Bysoth recalls being "designed by committee."*
**LEFT:** *Storyboards for various scenes from* Licence to Kill *including the infamous shark feeding sequence.*

for his more vicious fighting and determination. M is aware that the tragedy has clouded Bond's judgment, and makes allowances for him—Bond has not obeyed orders to go to Istanbul—but when Bond says he'll resign rather than give up the investigation, M snaps that the Secret Service "isn't a country club," revokes his license to kill, and demands his weapon. However, he stops other MI6 operatives from shooting Bond, although he alerts the Service's man in Isthmus (who tries to restrain Bond after the rogue agent interrupts a Hong Kong narcotics operation, and is killed by Sanchez's men for his troubles), then turns a blind eye to both Moneypenny and Q's less than surreptitious assistance. Despite Bond being directly responsible for the MI6 agent's death, M offers 007 his job back once Sanchez is dead.

His romantic entanglements are much less varied than normal—he becomes involved with Pam, and tries to refuse the approaches of Sanchez's girlfriend, Lupe Lamora (Talisa Soto)—a move that Dalton insisted on, since Fleming's Bond was a

**ABOVE:** *Robert Davi at the* Licence to Kill *photo call.* **LEFT:** *Timothy Dalton and co-star Carey Lowell arrive at the premiere for Dalton's second and final Bond outing.*

one-woman man (per assignment) in the books. It's hinted that seeing the Leiters' happiness reminds Bond of his own short-lived marriage—Felix stops Della from throwing the bouquet to him, and explains that Bond was once married "a long time ago." Bond is initially patronizing to Pam—"leave it to the professionals," he counsels her—but accepts her help when she shows her mettle. He's reluctant to accept Q's help, but grudgingly agrees that without his gadgets, he would have been dead years before.

He enjoys gambling, and drinks his martinis in his traditional way.

IN AN INTERVIEW IN 1989, Timothy Dalton said that he had "a feeling" that *Licence to Kill* would be the final Bond movie—"the end of the whole lot." It certainly was for him: legal problems regarding the sale of MGM, as well as a dispute over the television rights to the movie series, delayed any start on the third film in his contract for nearly three years, although a treatment for the movie was prepared in May 1990 by Alfonse M. Ruggiero Jr. and Michael G. Wilson (possibly based on Fleming's story "Property of a Lady," although this had been incorporated into *Octopussy*).

Dalton spent a lot of time during his tenure of the role trying to bring Ian Fleming's creation to life—from his first embittered comments to the Head of Station V about welcoming M dismissing him in *The Living Daylights* to his insistence on Bond being a one-woman man in *Licence to Kill*, he made his choices based on the character that Fleming created. Unfortunately, those producing the Bond films might not always have agreed, and Dalton's two movies showed a Bond who could be hurt, but still caught in the trappings of the superspy genre. He was no longer the invulnerable superhero walking through conflict and danger, like Connery or Moore, and the harshness of *Licence to Kill*—particularly its realistic violence—was not well-received by audiences or critics. Twenty years after Dalton's debut, Daniel Craig would present a similarly hardened interpretation of Bond to much greater acclaim.

Once the legal problems were resolved, work began again on a new script in 1993, with Michael France now hired as writer. At that point, Dalton was still under contract, but when pre-production continued beyond the end of 1993, Dalton decided not to continue, stating that the public had associated him with the role for eight years, and that was long enough. Pierce Brosnan's time had finally arrived.

# THE MUSIC OF JAMES BOND $007$

**M**usic has always been an essential part of the James Bond movie-going experience. All bar two of the movies—*Dr. No* and *OHMSS*—have had original songs playing over the start or end credits, with many of these becoming bona fide hits in their own right. There's as much interest in who is going to be writing and performing the theme song for the next Bond movie as there is in the actors playing the Bond girl or the villain. Monty Norman's distinctive "James Bond Theme," as arranged by John Barry, is one of the most recognizable pieces of music of the late twentieth century, and has featured in all of the official movies to date. It is noticeable by its absence in the renegade film, *Never Say Never Again*, whose star, Sean Connery, would later note: "That theme gives the audience a direct connection to Bond."

Although Shirley Bassey's rendition of "Goldfinger" is often seen as the moment when the music from the 007 films became the established

"sound" of the spy film genre, the first two films introduced key elements to the franchise.

*Dr. No* was scored by Monty Norman, a singer turned songwriter whose career prior to then had included the short-lived musical *Belle*, one of the backers of which was Cubby Broccoli, co-producer of the Bond films. Norman spent time on location in Jamaica, soaking in the atmosphere of the island

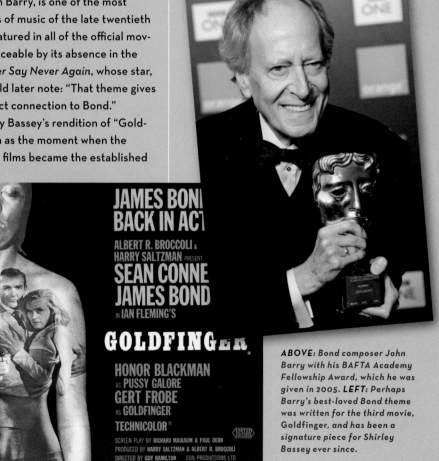

**ABOVE:** *Bond composer John Barry with his BAFTA Academy Fellowship Award, which he was given in 2005.* **LEFT:** *Perhaps Barry's best-loved Bond theme was written for the third movie, Goldfinger, and has been a signature piece for Shirley Bassey ever since.*

*ABOVE: Dame Shirley Bassey, who has appeared on the soundtracks of three Bond movies: Goldfinger, Diamonds are Forever, and Moonraker. BELOW RIGHT: The LP cover for the You Only Live Twice soundtrack; the version of Nancy Sinatra's title track on the record was different from that used in the movie.*

and writing tunes that could be played live on set. He composed "Underneath the Mango Tree" for the scene where Bond meets Honey Rider—in Fleming's novel, Bond joins in the refrain from a popular song that Honeychile is singing.

Bond's signature piece, however, didn't come to Norman until much later; under pressure to find a tune for the main titles, he dug out an old song, "Bad Sign, Good Sign," whose opening bars were then reworked by a young pop arranger, John Barry, into the familiar theme. This wasn't originally intended to appear in the soundtrack as often as it did, but editor Peter Hunt decided to use it "every time James Bond was about to do something, or something was about to happen"—a rule subsequently applied to every film. The "James Bond Theme" hit No. 13 in the UK singles chart; the *Dr. No* soundtrack album entered Billboard's American Top 100.

The sequel, *From Russia with Love*, used the "James Bond Theme" to great effect, as well as another piece Barry composed, "007," which made regular reappearances in Barry's scores for the series. Producers Broccoli and Harry Saltzman decided not to entrust the film's theme song to Barry, however, who was still seen as a promising youngster without a hit song to his name yet. Seeing how integral the music had been to *Dr. No*'s success, they decided to approach a "name" to compose the song, turning to Lionel Bart, whose *Oliver!* was a hit in London's West End and on Broadway. Crooner Matt Monro was hired to perform the song.

For *Goldfinger*, Barry was allowed to write the theme song, with lyrics written by Leslie Bricusse and Anthony Newley, and this also featured heavily within the underlying score for the film. Not that everyone was pleased with it: Harry Saltzman called it "the worst song I've ever heard in my goddamn life," but the worldwide public disagreed. Shirley Bassey's rendition—which required her to remove her bra to gain the freedom to hit the long note at the end in the studio—helped both the single and the album head toward the top of the

ORIGINAL MOTION PICTURE SOUNDTRACK

"YOU ONLY LIVE TWICE"

MUSIC COMPOSED, ARRANGED AND CONDUCTED BY
**JOHN BARRY**
TITLE SONG SUNG BY
**NANCY SINATRA**
LYRICS BY
**LESLIE BRICUSSE**

*HIGH FIDELITY* YOU ONLY LIVE TWICE • ORIGINAL MOTION PICTURE SOUNDTRACK • UNITED ARTISTS • UAL 4155

charts, with the soundtrack reaching No. 1 in the United States in March 1965.

Barry continued to score all of Sean Connery's official Bond movies, as well as George Lazenby's *OHMSS*, although none of the following four scores would attract as much attention as *Goldfinger* had. Attention was firmly on the songs and singers of the next two: heartthrob Tom Jones on *Thunderball*, and Nancy Sinatra on *You Only Live Twice*.

Jones' song was written hastily by Barry and lyricist Don Black after United Artists insisted that the original plan, to use a song entitled "Mr. Kiss Kiss, Bang Bang," wouldn't be acceptable to promote a film called *Thunderball*. Shirley Bassey recorded the original version of "Mr. Kiss Kiss, Bang Bang," but her version wasn't used in the final movie, and the music overall wasn't one of the aspects that received much attention, despite Jones' nine-second-long end note on "Thunderball."

Sinatra, whose father Frank was a friend of Cubby Broccoli, had established herself as a singer in her own right, and was asked to sing the love song that Leslie Bricusse and Barry had penned for *You Only Live Twice*, although the final version had to be pieced together from the twenty-five or so different takes in the studio.

*OHMSS* was a very different Bond film. Apart from starring a newcomer in the lead role, it also saw 007 fall in love and marry. To avoid trying to write a song entitled "On Her Majesty's Secret Service," Barry decided to use an instrumental theme under the main titles, and then invited the legendary Louis Armstrong to perform the film's main song, "We Have All the Time in the World," which appeared underneath a montage of Bond and Tracy di Vicenzo falling in love. The song received little recognition until it was used for a Guinness advertisement in the UK in 1994.

*Diamonds Are Forever* boasts an "over the top" title song, with "sleaziness [and] theatrical vulgarity," according to its lyricist, Don Black (something which didn't endear it to Harry Saltzman). Accompanying Connery's return as 007 was Shirley Bassey on vocals, singing a number which has become one of her own signature pieces, although most fans are unaware that there's a complete extra verse that was cut in the recording studio because the song was overrunning.

*Paul and Linda McCartney at the premiere for* Live and Let Die, *for which they sang the title track.*

*Live and Let Die* marked a sea change in the Bond movies, with Roger Moore taking the title role and John Barry nowhere to be seen. Former Beatle Paul McCartney didn't hold a grudge over the joke about the band in *Goldfinger* ("There are some things that just aren't done," Bond tells Jill Masterson. "Such as drinking Dom Pérignon '53 above a temperature of 38 degrees Fahrenheit. That's as bad as listening to the Beatles without earmuffs!"), and composed the theme, performing

*Roger Moore and Sheena Easton posing together to promote the film* For Your Eyes Only, *which features Easton's song of the same name.*

it with his band Wings—although initially Harry Saltzman had expected it to be sung by a female vocalist! The score was written by Beatles manager George Martin, with B.J. Arnau also singing the title number mid-movie: it became the first Bond song to be nominated for an Oscar, although it lost to "The Way We Were," from the movie of the same name. The song for *The Man with the Golden Gun* wasn't as well-received: a returning John Barry admitted that because he and Don Black had little time to write it, "the song just didn't happen." British star Lulu provided the vocals.

"Nobody Does It Better," proclaimed the theme for *The Spy Who Loved Me* (the movie title turns up within the lyrics), the first film produced solo by Cubby Broccoli. Barry was now a "tax exile," unable to work in the UK, so Broccoli turned to Marvin Hamlisch to provide the music for the new film. The Oscar-winning composer worked with his regular lyricist Carole Bayer Sager on the song, which was performed by Carly Simon.

Hamlisch updated the instrumentation heard in the score—notably on his action-packed reworking of Norman's "James Bond Theme," entitled "Bond 77"—and both song and score were Oscar-nominated.

The 1970s ended for Bond in outer space with the over-the-top *Moonraker*, for which both John Barry and Shirley Bassey returned, this time singing Hal David's lyrics. An earlier version, with words by Paul Williams, was going to be recorded by Frank Sinatra, but that never materialized; a version of it was laid down by Johnny Mathis, but the consensus was that the song wasn't working. Even the new piece wasn't one of Bond's most memorable.

Barry was one of the few elements not resurrected for the "back to basics" approach of *For Your Eyes Only*. The score (one of the longest composed for a Bond film) was written by Bill Conti, on Barry's recommendation, with the title song performed on screen by Scottish singer Sheena Easton, after main titles designer Maurice Binder became infatuated with her eyes. The song was Oscar-nominated and formed the centerpiece of an elaborate production number at the 1982 Academy Awards, at which Cubby Broccoli was honored.

Rival Bond films went head to head in 1983, but neither really exceled musically. The official film, *Octopussy*, saw Barry return, with the song "All Time High" co-written with *Evita*'s Tim Rice. Sung by Rita Coolidge, with the franchise's first specifically shot music video filmed at the Royal Pavilion (standing in for an Indian palace) in Brighton, England, it wasn't a chart hit.

Connery's *Never Say Never Again* featured a score by Michel Legrand, with the title song performed by Lani Hall (after Bonnie Tyler turned down the opportunity). Neither the score nor the theme worked as well as expected—the song was used over what should have been a tense opening to the movie, and the score was repurposed throughout the film.

Roger Moore's finale, *A View to a Kill*, saw Barry produce one of his weakest scores, but it was accompanied by one of the stronger Bond title themes, co-written with Barry and performed by Duran Duran. Their video for it—focusing on lead singer "Bon, Simon Le Bon"—incorporated footage from the Eiffel Tower chase in the film, and ensured that the song topped the charts in the US and reached the second spot in the UK. Duran Duran played the song as part of the Live Aid concert in 1985.

Barry enjoyed the collaboration with Duran Duran; however, the relationship with *The Living Daylights'* songmeisters, A-ha, was less congenial, resulting in the band reworking and remixing the song. The score featured Barry using synthesized drum tracks for the first time (Conti had used synths as instruments for *For Your Eyes Only*), and two extra songs were performed by the Pretenders, with Barry enjoying working with Chrissie Hynde on "Where Has Everybody Gone?" and end-title song "If There Was a Man." It was Barry's last contribution to a series in which he had been a key player.

Timothy Dalton's second and final 007 movie, *Licence to Kill*, was scored by Michael Kamen, then renowned for his work on the first *Die Hard* and *Lethal Weapon* movies, the sort of tough action films that *Licence Revoked* (as it was originally known) was attempting to emulate. Kamen's song featuring Vic Flick, the original "James Bond Theme" guitarist, and Eric Clapton was deemed unusable; Narada Michael Walden, Walter Afanasieff, and Jeffrey Cohen penned the opening theme, sung by Gladys Knight, while Patti LaBelle performed "If You Asked Me To" for the end credits. The video for

the former was created by Daniel Kleinman, who would go on to succeed Maurice Binder as main titles designer for the Brosnan era and beyond.

That new era began with a bit of a musical hiccup: Eric Serra's score for *GoldenEye* was very different from anything heard before in a Bond film. Where Tina Turner's anthemic title song, written by U2's Bono and the Edge, was the sort of brassy affair that brought back memories of "Goldfinger" or "Thunderball," Serra's music was avant-garde, mixing African sounds with percussion and a symphony orchestra. During the editing process it became clear that it wasn't working, and orchestrator John Altman was assigned to rescore the key tank chase through St. Petersburg, highlighting the "James Bond Theme."

The decision was therefore made to return Bond to his musical roots for *Tomorrow Never Dies*,

*Duran Duran's John Taylor and Simon Le Bon performing at Live Aid on July 13, 1985.*

*Jack White at the Royal World Premiere of* Quantum of Solace *on October 29, 2008.*

which marked the debut of David Arnold as composer. Arnold had arranged and produced an album of Bond covers, *Shaken and Stirred*, which both honored what had come before and presented a new take on it—"one foot in the 60s and one foot in the 90s," as Arnold later described it. (The video for "On Her Majesty's Secret Service" features a chase through the London Underground that pre-dates *Skyfall* by two decades!) A lot of musicians were approached about writing a song, with Sheryl Crow eventually chosen. Singer k.d. lang performed Don Black and Arnold's song "Surrender" over the end credits. Oddly, a third song—"Letter to Paris"—was written by Tommy Tallarico and performed by Elaine Paiva for the video game of the film!

Arnold's brand of updated Barry-esque music appeared in the next four movies, each time reflecting something of current musical trends along the way. *The World Is Not Enough*'s title song was performed by Shirley Manson and her band Garbage, and included lines from the script within the lyrics. A second song, "Only Myself to Blame," also by Black and Arnold, was recorded by Scott Walker but director Michael Apted elected to have an upbeat instrumental medley over the end titles instead. Garbage's song did well in the UK but not in the US, despite a major tie-in with MTV and an eclectic music video, set in *Goldfinger*'s year of release, 1964!

The Black/Arnold combination wasn't retained for the title song of Brosnan's farewell, *Die Another Day*; instead, it was written and sung by Madonna, who also took a small part in the movie (for which she received a Golden Raspberry Award nomination). The titles themselves were unusual, as they depicted Bond's torture over a prolonged period, and Madonna's theme, which out of context seems a complete aberration within the Bond canon, complements them. The song did not feature in Arnold's score, which included a lot of ethnic percussion to match the film's Korean setting.

When Daniel Craig assumed the mantle of Bond for *Casino Royale*, the song didn't feature the title at all: Chris Cornell's "You Know My Name" was co-written with David Arnold, and, according to the latter, was "built out of the DNA of the Bond theme . . . in a different order and in a different shape." The "James Bond Theme" itself doesn't turn up in the score until the very end of the movie, as indicated in the script, but Arnold used snippets of its bass line, reflecting Bond's progress toward becoming 007. Cornell's song didn't appear on the soundtrack album—perhaps explaining why it was one of the relatively few not to chart in the US.

There are many elements of *Quantum of Solace* that reflect the haste with which it was made, but not its music soundtrack. Arnold worked with director Marc Forster in a different way to his predecessors: rather than "spotting" the film, and choosing the areas which would be scored, Arnold composed pieces that reflected "the concept, the idea, the philosophy of the characters." Although there was considerable speculation that Amy Winehouse would provide the title theme, the singer's own demons prevented her from devoting the time necessary, and so the White Stripes' Jack White, a huge Bond fan, stepped in, penning the song "Another Way to Die" to be performed with Alicia Keys. The end music—"Crawl, End Crawl"—was an instrumental piece remixed by Kieran Hebden, aka Four Tet. The theme song was vilified as the worst Bond song ever.

Sam Mendes, the director of *Skyfall*, has a trusted team around him on his projects, including composer Thomas Newman, and it surprised no one to learn that Newton would be replacing Arnold for Daniel Craig's third film as Bond—least of all Arnold himself, who was already committed to the 2012 Olympics closing ceremony in London, and might not have had time anyway, given the delays to the film. The "James Bond Theme" at the end of the score comes from Arnold's recordings; Newman did his own arrangement, which appears as the track "Breadcrumbs" on the album. The title piece was sung by British artist Adele, who composed it with producer Paul Epworth; as well as reaching No. 2 in the UK, and eighth place in the US charts, it won a Golden Globe, a Brit Award and

an Oscar—the first 007 theme to do so. Newman will be returning to provide the score for Mendes's second Bond film, *SPECTRE*.

One other piece of music deserves mention—"The Look of Love," written by Burt Bacharach for the spoof version of *Casino Royale* in 1967. It turned up in the (much better) spoof *Austin Powers: International Man of Mystery* thirty years later—and became so synonymous with the 1960s that it nearly featured anachronistically in an episode of *Mad Men*'s fifth season!

*Adele with the Academy Award she won for the title track to the 2012 Daniel Craig movie* Skyfall, *which she co-wrote with Paul Epworth.*

# CHAPTER 009

# PIERCE BROSNAN: THE IRISH BOND

CRUELLY DEPRIVED OF HIS CHANCE TO PLAY JAMES BOND WHEN NBC ELECTED TO EXERCISE THEIR OPTION TO RENEW THE DETECTIVE SERIES *REMINGTON STEELE*— AT A POINT WHEN HIS SUCCESSION TO THE ROLE WAS ALL BUT ASSURED—PIERCE BROSNAN WOULD HAVE BEEN EXCUSED FOR BELIEVING THAT THE OPPORTUNITY HAD PASSED HIM BY. HOWEVER, WHEN TIMOTHY DALTON, THEN "THE BOND OF RECORD," ELECTED NOT TO CONTINUE IN THE PART, RESIGNING ON APRIL 11, 1994, BROSNAN BECAME THE 2-1 FAVORITE FOR THE ROLE WITH BRITISH BOOKMAKERS, WHILE WINNING VARIOUS AMERICAN POLLS FOR THE CHOICE OF THE NEXT 007.

The producers didn't need to screen test Brosnan; he had already jumped through all the hoops nearly a decade earlier. On June 1, 1994, he was offered the part; on June 7, he was formally announced as the fifth official screen James Bond.

Pierce Brendan Brosnan was born in May 1953 in Drogheda, County Louth, Ireland, moving to England in 1964—at which point he saw his first James Bond film,

**OPPOSITE:** *Pierce Brosnan casually dressed but ready for action as James Bond with the Aston Martin featured in GoldenEye.*

*Goldfinger*—and, after leaving school, began training as an illustrator before finding acting, and taking that up at the Drama Centre, London. His film career began with small roles in 1980, including *The Long Good Friday*, and after moving to America he became the star of *Remington Steele*. After that came to an end in 1987, he appeared in various film and TV series, including playing a British agent in TV movies based on the UNACO series of novels created by thriller writer Alistair MacLean.

## GOLDENEYE *(1995)*

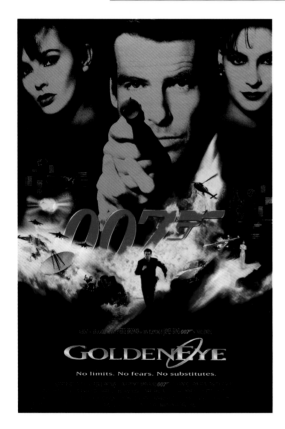

*The GoldenEye poster was the first to use photo manipulation, from images by Terry O'Neill, Keith Hamshere, and George Whitear.*

*GoldenEye* was not officially based on any of Ian Fleming's creations, bar 007 himself, although it was named after Fleming's house in Jamaica, where he wrote the stories. In an interesting twist, the film's introduction of a female M, played by Judi Dench, was reflected in the official continuation novels (see page 57).

It's 1986: Bond and 006, Alec Trevelyan (Sean Bean), raid a Soviet chemical factory, but 006 is captured and killed by Colonel Arkady Ourumov (Gottfried John). Nine years later, Bond stumbles upon a plot by Xenia Onatopp (Famke Janssen), a member of the Janus crime syndicate, to steal a Eurocopter Tiger helicopter, which can survive an electromagnetic pulse—such as the one that is shortly afterwards emitted by the GoldenEye satellite to destroy the bunker from where it had been controlled. The new M sends Bond to investigate, and he learns that Janus is run by a scarred Trevelyan. With help from former GoldenEye programmer Natalya Simonova (Izabella Scorupco), Bond escapes, and he learns that there is a second GoldenEye satellite, which Janus and Ourumov plan to use against the West. Bond kills Ourumov but Trevelyan escapes to Cuba; Bond and Simonova follow. They learn that Trevelyan is going to steal money electronically from the Bank of England before destroying its financial records and all other computer-held data in London with the GoldenEye. Bond prevents this, and lets Trevelyan fall to his death.

Early in *GoldenEye* the new M refers to Bond as "a sexist, misogynist dinosaur" and "a relic of the Cold War." He certainly still has an eye for the ladies, seducing the young woman sent by M to assess him, as well as engaging in verbal flirtation and violent foreplay (the violence from her side, it should be noted) with Xenia Onatopp, and having a more mature relationship with Natalya Simonova. Alec Trevelyan needles him that he is looking for forgiveness in the arms of different women "for all the dead ones you've failed to protect." (Bond has no answer to that charge.) His attitude, he claims, is "enjoy it—while it lasts" (an attitude M describes as cavalier), but he admits that he never learned to quit when he was ahead. He's verbally adept, frequently making comments with double meanings, and treating serious situations flippantly. He drinks vodka martini, shaken not stirred, as does Onatopp; when he's with M, he joins her in a glass of bourbon.

He hasn't spent long with the new M, and has yet to come to respect her, regarding her as a "bean counter" more interested in numbers than her agents' instincts. However, he is impressed by her stated willingness to send him to his death if necessary, and claims that he won't let the mission get personal. (The lack of respect seems to go both ways at this point.)

He flirts with Moneypenny (played, as throughout Brosnan's tenure, by Samantha Bond), claiming that he's never seen her "after hours"—Moneypenny points out that he's never "had" her either. His attitude to Q is more like a

**TOP:** *Izabella Scorupco and Peirce Brosnan on set with the BMW Z3 that made a brief appearance in GoldenEye.*
**ABOVE:** *Judi Dench made her first appearance as M in GoldenEye; although she would appear in seven Bond films in total, she played two different versions of the Secret Service head.*

*Sean Bean (right) and Pierce Brosnan (left) perch on the Aston Martin hood for the GoldenEye press call.*

kid in a candy store, looking round at all the goodies on display rather than listening to the briefing.

He's shocked when he meets Trevelyan again, believing him to have been killed, and he's angry at him for his betrayal; Trevelyan knew Bond wouldn't join his plan, since he is too loyal to Queen and country. Trevelyan's actions get to Bond, though, and he admits to Natalya that he has to be cold about what he needs to do, in order to stay alive—although she points out that this also means he stays alone. When he kills Trevelyan, it's personal—not "for England," but "for me."

Bond is adept at driving pretty much anything that comes to hand—a motorcycle, a small plane, a motorboat, and even a Russian tank—and has an Aston Martin DB5 once more, which has a place for a bottle of champagne and two glasses. He's accomplished at baccarat (despite Onatopp's sarcastic comments about his prowess) and is up to date on Russian crime-syndicate members, as well as the history of the Lienz Cossacks. He's been inside Russia several times, on one such occasion providing underworld kingpin Valentin Zukovsky (Robbie Coltrane) with his limp and stealing his girl.

He's not up to date with computer technology and parlance, trusting that Natalya knows what she's doing, even if he doesn't, although he's able to recognize what Trevelyan is up to with the banking system quickly.

## TOMORROW NEVER DIES *(1997)*

Brosnan's second movie, *Tomorrow Never Dies*, suffered from an unusual lack of preparation by the Bond team; filming began before the script was ready, and there were various disputes on set (unusually, these problems were all documented in the official book on the making of the film). First unit filming started on April 1, 1997; the film opened on December 9, and while the first half of the movie holds together pretty well, the second feels rushed. Once more, this is a completely original story, with only the set-up derived from Fleming's novels.

American techno-terrorist Henry Gupta (Ricky Jay) buys a GPS encoder from a Russian arms bazaar; the device is used by media baron Elliot Carver (Jonathan Pryce) to ramp up tensions between China and the United Kingdom. A British frigate is sunk by Carver's stealth ship and a Chinese fighter jet is shot down. Bond is given 48 hours to investigate Carver, whose media empire has released details of the attacks suspiciously early. Bond, who has previously had a relationship with Carver's wife, Paris (Teri Hatcher), steals the encoder back, but Carver has his wife killed for rekindling her relationship with 007. Bond manages to escape and investigates the wreck of the frigate, working with Chinese agent Wai Lin (Michelle Yeoh). Both are captured but escape and board Carver's stealth boat to prevent him from using a British missile he has stolen from the frigate to precipitate a war.

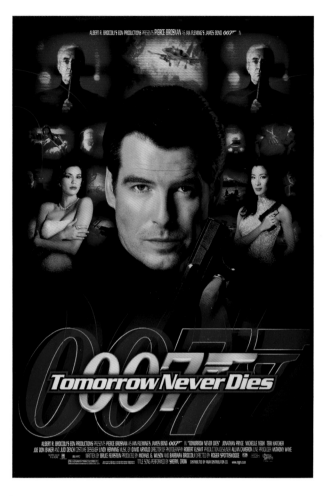

*Keith Hamshere and George Whitear produced an appropriately media-filled image for* Tomorrow Never Dies.

*Tomorrow Never Dies* begins with Bond demonstrating his training—remaining concealed until necessary, close-quarters fighting, being able to identify weaponry quickly, improvising as required, and knowing how to fly a foreign power's planes. He also shows an unusual antipathy to smoking ("filthy habit").

He's as suave and charming as ever with his Danish teacher (demonstrating he's a cunning linguist, even if he can't use Chinese ideographs on a laptop), and he flirts with Moneypenny. The relationship with M is now business-like, and she has no qualms about ordering him to remind Paris Carver of their previous relationship—

*The key cast of* Tomorrow Never Dies *gathers at the premiere. From left to right: Jonathan Pryce, Götz Otto, Michelle Yeoh, and Pierce Brosnan.*

which clearly didn't end well, since her first reaction to seeing Bond is to slap him and remind him that he said he would be "right back." They become lovers again, and Bond is clearly grief-stricken when he finds her body—he's lying when he tells Dr. Kaufman (Vincent Schiavelli), Paris' killer, that killing him is just business for him, too. As with Alec Trevelyan's death in *GoldenEye*, he takes a personal pleasure in "giving the people what they want" and allowing Elliot Carver to be killed by a giant screw. He is professional with Chinese agent Wai Lin—even if Carver thinks he's being "romantic" when Bond tells her they will finish the mission together—until the climax of the story, when he has to kiss her to pass oxygen, but then continues kissing her once they are on the surface of the ocean.

He can be adolescent in behavior, with Q growling at him to "grow up" when he shows off his prowess with the remote control for his BMW car. Even in the midst of danger, he can see the humor— when the tires on his car automatically re-inflate, a broad grin crosses his face—and, perhaps to release the tension, makes a quip after many fights.

# THE WORLD IS NOT ENOUGH (1999)

Brosnan's third movie followed two years later. *The World Is Not Enough* derived its title from the Bond family motto, as established by Ian Fleming in *OHMSS*. Bond explains its significance to Elektra King (Sophie Marceau) when she is in the middle of torturing him toward the end of the film; she says she could have offered him the world, and he offers the motto as a quip. Like the previous Brosnan movies, there are few plot connections to Fleming's work, bar the character of 007, although the concept of kidnapping M was at the heart of the first official continuation novel, Robert Markham's *Colonel Sun* (which was also mined for material for the next film, *Die Another Day*).

Sir Robert King, an old friend of M, is assassinated within MI6 headquarters, and Bond is injured while chasing the assassin, who kills herself. He is assigned to look after King's daughter Elektra, who years earlier was kidnapped by former KGB agent Renard (Robert Carlyle); M advised Sir Robert not to pay the ransom. Elektra is constructing an oil pipeline in Azerbaijan, and, although it seems as if her chief of security is working with Renard, it transpires that Elektra herself is now his ally. Elektra kidnaps M, and with the help of nuclear scientist Dr. Christmas Jones (Denise Richards) 007 needs to rescue M as well as prevent Renard from using stolen Russian nuclear material to cause an explosion on a submarine in Istanbul harbor.

**TOP:** *Pierce Brosnan as Bond in one of the character portrait posters released for* The World Is Not Enough. **ABOVE:** *The two villainous ladies of* The World Is Not Enough: *Maria Cucionotta and Sophie Marceau.*

Bond's coolness in dangerous situations continues to be at the fore, as does his penchant for wordplay—in fact, there are many times, particularly when he's talking to Christmas Jones, when he cannot resist bad puns, making him sound rather adolescent. He can be nonchalant, checking his tie is straight while underwater in the middle of the boat chase at the start of the movie, and is charming to the ladies, seducing Doctor Warmflash (Serena Scott Thomas) into giving him a clean bill of health. He ends up in bed with Elektra, despite direct orders not to do so, and eventually sleeps with Christmas (making the inevitable jokes about her name).

His relationship with M is initially more relaxed than has been seen on screen previously, joining his superior officer and Sir Robert for a social drink, but he is willing to challenge her when necessary, particularly when he thinks, correctly, that she's trying to keep him off the operation. The bantering continues with Moneypenny, and there's an affection for Q which is warmer than previously—Bond is concerned when it seems as if Q is hinting that he's about to retire. (Actor Desmond Llewelyn's death shortly afterward gives this scene a particular poignancy.) He's not so impressed with Q's new assistant, "R" (John Cleese), who is equally unimpressed with "the legendary 007 wit—or at least half of it." Robbie Coltrane returns as Valentin Zukovsky, and their relationship has been strong enough that the Russian gangster turned caviar seller and nightclub owner trusts 007 when he presents evidence of the impending nuclear attack on Istanbul. Indeed, as he's dying, he helps the agent one last time by shooting his bonds (the script suggests at that point that they are "comrades in arms," and Zukovsky dies with "the merest of smiles").

Bond can adapt to any vehicle quickly (the script suggests he simply "presses something red" to make the "Q-boat" launch), and is an expert skier. He relies on Christmas Jones to deal with the nuclear devices, but he knows what he's doing in a submarine, even a Russian one. He keeps calm under pressure—whether it's in the aftermath of an avalanche, or when stuck with a nuclear bomb about to explode—and he can still make a quip when he is being tortured. He hates being betrayed (perhaps a legacy of his relationship with Alec Trevelyan in *GoldenEye*), and he is cold when he delivers the *coup de grâce* to Elektra.

# DIE ANOTHER DAY (2002)

The world had changed forever by the time the next 007 movie hit our screens in November 2002. Fourteen months earlier, exactly four months before shooting on the new film started on January 11, planes piloted by al-Qaeda terrorists destroyed the World Trade Center in New York and caused damage to the Pentagon. There was a new enemy at large, and the larger-than-life heroics of 007 didn't sit as well as they had.

The first Bond movie of the twenty-first century was Pierce Brosnan's last. *Die Another Day* was the twentieth in the official series, and there were considerable nods to the past throughout the film—from the recreation of iconic shots, with Halle Berry rising from the water in a bikini as Ursula Andress had done forty years earlier, to blatant references, such as Q (now played by John Cleese) pointing out that he believed Bond's new watch to be the "twentieth" he had been given. It received a mixed reception: director Lee

*The poster for Pierce Brosnan's final movie as 007 gives equal prominence to Halle Berry's CIA agent Jinx.*

Tamahori's decision to use computer-generated imagery for some of the stunt work was not popular (one of the films' many claims to fame was their preference for practical stunts), and some of the gadgets, such as a car that could turn invisible, were too outlandish, with even Roger Moore commenting negatively about them, while acknowledging that he took the character into outer space. Brosnan himself has subsequently agreed with many of the criticisms.

The story derives some of its elements from Fleming's third Bond novel, *Moonraker*—a weapon hidden in plain sight that is going to bring devastation—as well as a small amount from the first continuation novel, Robert Markham's *Colonel Sun*. In that novel, it's M who is tortured by the villain; in this, it's 007 himself.

James Bond is on a mission in North Korea, investigating Colonel Tan-Sun Moon (Will Yun Lee), who is trading weapons for conflict diamonds. After his cover is blown, Bond is chased by Moon, who is apparently killed; Bond is imprisoned for fourteen months by Moon's father, a general. After Bond is traded for Moon's henchman Zao (Rick Yune), he is told he's a security risk because he must have betrayed secrets during his imprisonment. Determined to clear his name, Bond follows Zao to Cuba, where he teams up with NSA agent Giacinta "Jinx" Johnson (Halle Berry) and finds a gene-therapy clinic, where people have their appearances altered. The trail leads him to Gustav Graves (Toby Stephens), an apparently altruistic billionaire who has created a satellite that can focus solar energy. Graves is, in fact, an altered Colonel Moon, and he plans to use the Icarus satellite to enable North Korean forces to invade the south. He's been helped by MI6 agent Miranda Frost (Rosamund Pike), who betrayed Bond and the secrets. Bond and Jinx kill Frost and Graves and prevent war.

After two films in which Brosnan's Bond has been the one betrayed, in his final appearance it happens once again, but this time it is he who is regarded with suspicion by the intelligence agencies—he's treated with contempt by the CIA's Damian Falco (Michael Madsen), and even M believes it's possible that Bond cracked under interrogation. In fact, Bond's inner steel is displayed more than ever before: we see him resist torture for fourteen months, but he is still able to make a feeble quip when General Moon arrives to take him from his cell. He is confident enough in his ability to withstand torture to get rid of his cyanide capsule "years ago." The medical examination carried out after he's been traded shows a standard pulse (72) and blood pressure (120 over 80). His internal organs are unaffected by the poisonings and antidotes he's ingested, but his liver is showing signs of other damage (which persuades the doctors that it's definitely 007!). He has considerable control over his body functions, able to fake a cardiac arrest and recover from near-death quickly enough to take out those sent after him.

He's a skilled fencer, indulging in some light combat with the trainer at Graves's club, Verity (Madonna), before an escalating duel with Gustav Graves nearly leads to bloodshed. He's a good surfer, and is able to pilot a Switchblade—a "Programmable High Altitude Single Soldier Transport" craft—as well as a hovercraft.

As far as sexual relationships go, he's delighted to relieve his frustrations with a Chinese masseuse shortly after his release, and he has a highly charged relationship with Jinx—we even see some of his sexual technique. Miranda Frost is determined to keep him at arm's length—unsuccessfully—summing Bond up to M as "a blunt instrument whose primary method is to provoke and confront" (a fair assessment of Brosnan's 007), and telling Bond himself that she knows all about him: "Sex for dinner, death for breakfast." She's not the only one to present Bond with others' perceptions of him: when his true identity is revealed, Gustav Graves tells 007 that he chose to model himself on the details of Bond's persona. "That unjustifiable swagger," Graves comments. "Your crass quips—a defense mechanism concealing such inadequacy." Bond's propensity to quip increases as he feels more comfortable back in his role at the Secret Service—and doesn't stop even in the face of death at Frost and Graves's hands.

Inevitably, the relationship between M and Bond suffers; the Head of the Service advised Sir Robert King not to bargain for Elektra in the previous film, and here she tells Bond bluntly that if she had her way, he'd still be in North Korea. However, she will not countenance him going after the person he says betrayed him, and she

*Pierce Brosnan with his final Bond leading ladies, Rosamund Pike and Halle Berry.*

intends to send him to the evaluation center in the Falkland Islands, with his double-o status rescinded since he is now "no use to anyone." However, she denies to the CIA that she gave Bond any assistance with his escape, although she's perfectly prepared to use him once she realizes that he's on Graves's trail.

Bond claims to M that he's not prepared to compromise his principles (which is a bit rich given that he was happy to work with Chinese intelligence to find Zao, arriving at a Hong Kong hotel to make contact with its manager, who is also a Chinese spy), and is testy when he asks her if it's okay now for him to get on with his job. This testiness starts to disappear when he meets the new quartermaster—the old "R"—and his childish behavior returns, constantly fiddling with everything. Although we see Moneypenny's feelings toward Bond expressed in a virtual-reality sequence at the end of the film, the characters don't cross paths in the film.

In the publicity rounds accompanying the release of *Die Another Day*, Pierce Brosnan informed CNN that he had already been asked to make his fifth movie as the secret agent, but eventually the Broccolis decided to move in a different direction, rebooting the Bond saga with a new actor in the lead, and removing many of the central planks of the series. There were also plans afoot to produce a solo movie involving Halle Berry's character, Jinx; these too did not materialize as planned.

Brosnan gave audiences a lighter-weight version of Bond after the attempted seriousness of the Timothy Dalton films, bringing back the quips and the sexual profligacy that were more in line with Connery or Moore's era, rather than Dalton or, indeed, Fleming's original. Initially, there were some attempts, at least in *GoldenEye* and to an extent *Tomorrow Never Dies*, to show some of Bond's inner feelings, but in his latter two movies, Brosnan was much closer to Moore's superhero secret agent known by everyone—a far cry from the hardened agent of the novels. On the rare occasions that he showed his steel, Brosnan was as strong as Connery in the role; however, for most of the time, he simply looked the part.

Some of them want to destroy the world. Others want to rule one or more countries, either openly or covertly, by controlling global media or through terrorist organizations. Some are motivated by politics, others by greed. Some are undoubtedly insane; others only seem that way to those not within their select circle. They are the men and women after whom James Bond is sent.

The image of the white-cat-stroking, disfigured maniac, with his high-tech head-quarters hidden in the heart of a volcano, has almost become a shorthand image for the archetypal Bond movie villain, even if the person in question, Ernst Stavro Blofeld, only appeared in seven films and three novels. That's a tribute to Donald Pleasence's unforgettable performance in *You Only Live Twice* (and he was a last-minute replacement for the actor originally cast, Jan Werich), and the strength of the character created in the novel *Thunderball*, in which Blofeld is the shadowy head of SPECTRE (the Special Executive for Counter-Intelligence, Terrorism, Revenge and Extortion).

SPECTRE loomed behind the scenes of all of the Connery and Lazenby movies—Dr. No, Kronsteen, Rosa Klebb, and Goldfinger all worked for them (rather than being Russian agents, as they were in Fleming's original stories)—and their final appearance in the twentieth-century films was a brief one by an unnamed Blofeld at the start of *For Your Eyes Only*. They were operative in a number of Jim Lawrence's newspaper strips, run by a mysterious Madame Spectra who died in the story "Doomcrack." Blofeld's daughter Nena then reac-

tivated the organization in John Gardner's second Bond novel, *For Special Services*; she was replaced as chief by Tamil Rahani, who targeted Bond in two further adventures. They didn't appear in the first three Daniel Craig movies, but their return is central to the twenty-fourth film, which is named after them. It will be interesting to see how they

*Donald Pleasence as Ernst Stavro Blofeld, complete with white cat, ready to face James Bond in* You Only Live Twice.

are linked with the Quantum organization featured in Daniel Craig's first two films (as demonstrated in the trailer), and how the scriptwriters envisage a twenty-first-century SPECTRE.

Ian Fleming had a gift for creating larger-than-life characters—not just James Bond himself, but those he battled. Many of them are far more outlandish in the original stories than their film versions: Sir Hugo Drax in Fleming's *Moonraker* is the product of failed plastic surgery, with a "tissue of shining puckered skin" covering "most of the right half of his face" and a right eye considerably larger than the left. (Christopher Wood tones down the description in his novelization, but it's still closer to Fleming's character than Michael Lonsdale's appearance.) Goldfinger is only five feet tall in the novel, and "it was as if [he] had been put together with bits of other people's bodies." Dr. No "looked like a giant venomous-worm wrapped in grey tinfoil." The comic strip adaptations, which started to appear long before the movies were produced, drew upon Fleming's word-pictures to provide a rogues' gallery of grotesques.

In addition to physical deformities of some sort, Fleming's villains had psychological flaws: Le Chiffre renames himself because he believes he is just a number on a document; Drax seeks revenge on the British; Goldfinger has a fetish for gold; Red Grant, the SMERSH assassin working for Rosa Klebb in *From Russia, with Love*, is a psychopath, affected by the full moon. Blofeld may have started off with a desire to control the world through

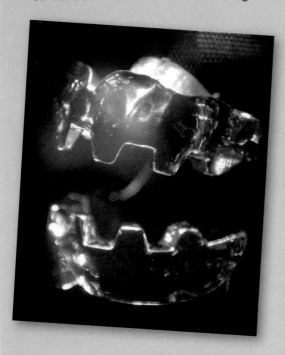

SPECTRE, but he ended up creating a Garden of Death on a Japanese island, filled with plants and creatures that provided agonizing ends for those who visited.

Of course, not all of Bond's literary foes were megalomaniacs: the Spang brothers—the diamond smugglers in *Diamonds Are Forever*—were ruthless businessmen, as was Colonel von Hammerstein, whom Bond encountered in "For Your Eyes Only." Sol Horowitz and Sluggsy Morant were small-time thugs who chose the wrong day to try to commit arson in *The Spy Who Loved Me*. However, those who haven't read the books won't know who these characters are: when the novels were adapted for the screen, they weren't deemed sufficiently threatening to the globetrotting screen persona of Bond.

As the films grew ever further away from Fleming's originals—a process that really began with *You Only Live Twice*, which bears little resemblance to the source novel—so the villains became ever larger. Scaramanga in *The Man with the Golden Gun* is a world-class assassin, not a small-time Caribbean hitman; Drax doesn't want to fire a rocket at London, but to destroy all of humanity.

There were occasional efforts to bring things down to earth: *For Your Eyes Only* notably featured smaller-scale villainy for the most part; *Licence to Kill* pits Bond against a drug-smuggler, Franz Sanchez. However, the stakes were higher during Pierce Brosnan's time: ex-MI6 agent Alec Trevelyan's plans and motivations in *GoldenEye* echoed those in the novel of *Goldfinger*; Elliot Carver was happy to start a war to increase his media empire's circulation figures in *Tomorrow Never Dies*; Renard would happily set off a nuclear bomb in Istanbul to ensure his lover's oil became

*The stainless steel teeth adopted by Richard Kiel to play the part of Jaws in* The Spy Who Loved Me *and* Moonraker.

more valuable in *The World Is Not Enough*; Gustav Graves (aka Colonel Tan-Sun Moon) wanted to start a war in Korea in *Die Another Day*. The Quantum organization that featured in the first two Daniel Craig films was highly reminiscent of a less belligerent SPECTRE, but Raoul Silva returned us to the villainous archetypes of old with his physical deformities and warped reasoning in *Skyfall*.

Fleming's literary heirs have also latched on to that portion of the Bond mythos with gusto. Robert Markham gave us the sadistic Colonel Sun; Christopher Wood fleshed out both Karl Stromberg and his comic book–like sidekick Jaws into more three-dimensional characters in his novel *James Bond, The Spy Who Loved Me*. Young Bond's adversaries in Charlie Higson and Steve Cole's books all suffer from mental or physical defects. John Gardner, Raymond Benson and the single-novel writers provided characters with a wealth of ailments—although, of course, all would be horrified to think that they were suggesting that suffering from such conditions automatically means you're going to become a threat to Queen and country!

Javier Bardem, who played Silva in *Skyfall*, summed up the difficult balancing act that every Bond writer has faced. "We have to find the middle ground between reality and fiction. The Bond

*Mathieu Amalric looking rather more suave than he does as the unpleasant Dominic Greene in* Quantum of Solace.

villain is in itself a genre," he told the *Miami Beach Examiner*. "People expect the Bond villain to be somebody that's a little bit out there, and we have to do that without losing the sensation of belonging to the Earth."

# DANIEL CRAIG:
# THE BLOND BOND

R EADING THE NEGATIVE HEADLINES THAT GREETED THE NEWS OF THE CASTING OF PIERCE BROSNAN'S REPLACEMENT AS 007, YOU WOULD HAVE BEEN EXCUSED FOR THINKING THAT BARBARA BROCCOLI AND MICHAEL G. WILSON, THE EXECUTIVE PRODUCERS OF THE BOND SERIES, HAD LOST THEIR MINDS. THE FACT THAT DANIEL CRAIG DIDN'T PRECISELY MATCH THE PHYSICAL DESCRIPTION OF 007 GIVEN IN IAN FLEMING'S BOOKS—HE'S SHORTER THAN THE AUTHOR DESCRIBES, AND HIS HAIR IS BLONDER—SEEMED TO SOME TO INDICATE THAT THERE WAS NO POSSIBILITY HE COULD PLAY BOND PROPERLY. THE SUCCESS OF *CASINO ROYALE*, *QUANTUM OF SOLACE*, AND *SKYFALL* WOULD PROVE THE NAYSAYERS WRONG.

When the EON team decided that they were going to go back to the beginning and "reboot" the series—i.e. wipe the slate clean of all past continuity and the baggage that had accreted over the past forty years—it seemed sensible to recast the part. (Although Judi Dench continued to play M, it's clear from the films that she is a new version of the same character.) Pierce Brosnan accepted the news gracefully, and the hunt was on for the next Bond.

*Health and safety requirements meant Daniel Craig's first appearance in public as Bond at St. Katherine Docks, London, was in a life-preserver.*

According to Barbara Broccoli, Daniel Craig was their first choice; however, the Bond franchise being such a major money spinner, the studio "wanted us to see everybody." For Broccoli, "When Craig is on the screen you can't take your eyes off him . . . you think, 'My God, he has such presence and such charisma.'" Michael G. Wilson commented that over two hundred actors were considered for the role, and during the audition process *Variety* reported that Craig, Henry Cavill (who would go on to play Superman in the Man of Steel movies), *ER*'s Goran Visnjic, and future *Avatar* star Sam Worthington were the key four in contention. *Casino Royale* director Martin Campbell later noted that he believed Cavill was Craig's only serious competition, but was deemed too young at twenty-two to play the part, despite the nature of the role. (Cavill went on to play a different character created by Ian Fleming: Napoleon Solo, *The Man from U.N.C.L.E.*, in Guy Ritchie's 2015 reboot of the classic 1960s spy series.)

Craig was initially reluctant to come aboard, and Broccoli and Wilson had to "woo him" for the role, but eventually, once he saw the script, he signed up. On October 14, 2005, he was announced as the new 007—although there were snide reports in the press about the health-and-safety requirement that meant he had to travel to the press conference in a life preserver, and headlines such as "The Bland Bond" from British tabloid newspapers.

Daniel Wroughton Craig was born on March 2, 1968, and started acting at the age of six in school plays. After leaving school, he went to the National Youth Theatre in London, and later graduated from the Guildhall School of Music and Drama in 1991. His stage career included appearances as Joe in the National Theatre's production of the AIDS drama *Angels in America* in 1993, and he was one of *Our Friends in the North*, the prestigious BBC drama production in 1996—which first brought him to the attention of Broccoli, who considered that he was "destined to become a star." His career continued on both big and small screens, with roles in the historical drama *Elizabeth*, the Evelyn Waugh adaptation *Sword of Honour*, and opposite Angelina Jolie in *Tomb Raider*. Sam Mendes cast him as Paul Newman's son in the 1930s gangster movie *Road to Perdition* (after an audition both men describe as awful), released in 2002, and prior to donning the Bond mantle, he appeared in Matthew Vaughn's contemporary gangster film *Layer Cake*, as well as Steven Spielberg's *Munich*—which brought him into contact with real members of the Secret Services.

Craig wasn't interested in playing the sort of jokey Bond that had appeared in the series periodically—as he pointed out forcefully, *"Austin Powers* fucked it." Mike Myers's trilogy of initially affectionate Bond spoofs released between 1997 and 2002 meant that the genuine 007 couldn't send up situations anymore. Craig saw a darkness in the original Bond stories, with a sense of black humor, and although his Bond was sometimes criticized for being too serious, like Timothy Dalton, he went back to the Ian Fleming novels for inspiration. He also consciously played the part differently from all of his predecessors, as he felt they had from each other, and in 2008 he commented: "The question I keep asking myself while playing the role is, 'Am I the good guy or just a bad guy who works for the good side?' Bond's role, after all, is that of an assassin when you come down to it."

## CASINO ROYALE (2006)

Craig's debut movie as Bond was a new version of Ian Fleming's first novel. The rights to *Casino Royale* had been sold separately from the rest of Fleming's work, but MGM, the studio behind the Bond series, acquired them from Sony in 1999 after trading them for the rights to the Marvel Comics character Spider-Man. Although a 1954 American TV adaptation had been moderately faithful to the

*Empire Design's poster for the rebooted series hints at how different this Bond will be from his predecessors.*

*Hands across the ocean: Judi Dench (M) with Jeffrey Wright (CIA agent Felix Leiter) at the premiere of* Casino Royale.

beats of the story, few were aware of it (see pages 175–178), and *Casino Royale* was primarily known for the over-the-top 1967 version. The darker Bond that Fleming described—the one who would consider marriage to a fellow agent, but then describe her as "the bitch" once her treachery has been revealed—had never been seen on screen.

The script, by Paul Haggis, and Neal Purvis & Robert Wade, follows Fleming's tale more closely than first impressions might suggest—the sequence where Bond races after Patrice to prevent him from destroying the airliner and manages to place the explosive on the bomber himself takes its inspiration from a short scene in the book where one of the Bulgars kills himself with his own explosive (a reworking of the scene which was added to the script during filming). Of course, it's done on a much larger scale—and it's an unnamed organization (later revealed to be Quantum) for whom Le Chiffre is working, rather than the Russian SMERSH.

James Bond is promoted to the 00 section and given his license to kill. His pursuit of a bomb maker in Madagascar puts him on the trail of Alex Dimitrios (Simon Abkarian), an associate of international terrorist financier Le Chiffre (Mads Mikkelsen). Bond foils Le Chiffre's plan to destroy an airliner, which would have allowed one of his clients to make a huge profit on the stock exchange, and Le Chiffre sets up a high-stakes poker game at the Casino Royale in Montenegro to recoup his money. With the aid of British Treasury agent Vesper Lynd (Eva Green) and CIA agent Felix Leiter (Jeffrey Wright in the first of two appearances in the role), Bond beats Le Chiffre, despite an attempt on his life. The terrorist then captures Bond and tortures him for the password to the Swiss account where the winnings are held; however, Le Chiffre is killed by Mr. White, one of his bosses (Jesper Christensen). In love, Bond and Vesper travel to Venice, but when Bond learns that the money has not been returned to the Treasury, he realizes Vesper is a double agent, and follows her and her fellow agents into a building which collapses. Vesper allows herself to drown. Bond pursues Mr. White and the film ends with him shooting White beside Lake Como.

Forget everything you know about the suave, sophisticated agent of the twenty films up to now. Daniel Craig's Bond is a completely new incarnation: younger, ruthless, and—as demonstrated very early on in the film—a savage fighter who will use everything at his disposal to survive, including the washbasin against a wall. He hasn't killed prior to the events shown in the film: Dryden's contact, Fisher, is the first person who dies at his hands, and it's clear that Bond feels it—although, as Dryden (Malcolm Sinclair) assures him, he finds the second kill is considerably easier. It doesn't mean that he's become a killing machine; after he kills an African warlord's thug in a violent struggle, he takes some time to get his head back in the game.

Bond has incredible stamina: he's able to keep up with a parkour runner over a considerable distance and then haul him across the yard of a foreign embassy. He can withstand severe poisoning and almost die from cardiac arrest—and then go straight back into a poker game as if nothing has happened!

He can drive pretty much anything, including a construction digger and a gasoline tanker, and he doesn't suffer from vertigo—or, if he does, he's very good at disguising it, fighting the bomber on the top of a girder high above the ground, and making the leap from one beam to another.

Mads Mikkelsen, Caterina Murino, and Daniel Craig at the Casino Royale premiere.

He reacts instinctively to situations in front of him rather than considering the ramifications of his actions, and feels that one less bomber in the world is a good idea, even if bringing him in alive might help capture more than one. This attitude puts him at odds with M on more than one occasion—she considers that she might have promoted him too quickly, suggesting that he has had something of a meteoric rise within the Secret Intelligence Service. (Interestingly, the original script suggested that the title sequence—rather than going with the playing-card motif finally adopted—showed photos from Bond's CV, "including his stint in the SAS.") He is, however, self-aware enough to realize that 00 agents have a short life expectancy, and later he recognizes that it was his impatience—and maybe even arrogance—that allowed Le Chiffre to counter-bluff him. He's reckless, but not suicidal—although after he fails to beat Le Chiffre at the poker table, he is willing to risk his own life to take the financier out.

He can pick locks, and is adept with computers—he is able to get hold of M's real name, as well as her login and password, for the MI6 secure website. He is an expert at cards, and is able to win Dimitrios's 1964 Aston Martin from him, as well as defeat Le Chiffre at Casino Royale—this he achieves by being able to read people's "tells," the specific way they react in certain situations, such as when they're bluffing. He does have some sophisticated tastes: he knows precisely how he likes his dry martini to be prepared (although, under pressure, he couldn't give a damn if it's shaken or stirred), and eats lobster and caviar with Vesper after the victory over Le Chiffre. Life or death situations bring out the black humor in him, notably when he's being tortured by Le Chiffre.

Bond admits to Solange (Dimitrios's wife, played by Caterina Murino) that he prefers relationships with married women, since it "keeps things simple." As Solange fears, Bond uses her without a second thought to get to Dimitrios, something he finds hard to regret even after her death—a point M recognizes when she comments that staying emotionally detached won't be difficult for Bond.

His relationship with Vesper doesn't start well after he makes some well-educated guesses about her to demonstrate his ability to read people. In return, she guesses that Bond went to Oxford, and before that, he was at a fee-paying school where his friends didn't let him forget that he wasn't from a moneyed background. Bond only reacts when she says he is an orphan, and Vesper further deduces that he's ex-SAS and the sort of maladjusted young man MI6 recruit to serve Queen and country. She

thinks he sees women as "disposable pleasures rather than meaningful pursuits"—so she's not going to get involved with him, even though he has a "perfectly formed arse." Bond doesn't correct any of her comments.

After this prickly start, Bond is able to tease her to a degree—claiming that her alias is Miss Stephanie Broadchest—and reassures her that she's not his type: she's single. He's able to judge her dress size and what will suit her, even if his own taste in dinner jackets isn't as impeccable as it could be. It's clear that he's not as emotionally detached as he would like to be when he sits in the shower with her as she tries to come to terms with the sudden deaths she's just witnessed, and during his convalescence he admits to himself, and her, that she has stripped him of his emotional armor and he belongs to her. Perhaps because he can't find her "tell," he falls in love with her, and is willing to quit the Secret Service to be with her. He knows that his job is soul-destroying, and he wants to get out while some of his is still intact. However, when he learns of her betrayal, and despite the fact that she commits suicide, the hard exterior re-forms, and he admits to M that he now trusts no one. He has learned his lesson, and, as the script notes, M has "sacrificed a man to create a spy."

## QUANTUM OF SOLACE (2008)

Craig's debut was widely praised, with many of his detractors admitting that he had been considerably better than they had feared. Although his performance in his second film was as well-received, the movie itself wasn't. *Quantum of Solace*, directed by Marc Forster, was by far the shortest 007 film of recent times, and seemed to take the series in an even dourer direction. This was in part because,

as Craig later admitted, they had to start shooting without a completed script (not the first time this had happened—*Tomorrow Never Dies* suffered from the same problem), and because of a strike by the Writers Guild of America, only Craig and Forster could rework scenes.

The title derives from a short story in the *For Your Eyes Only* collection, an oddity in the canon, as it's a story that Bond is told at a dinner party. No element of it is used in the film, although the final scene—where Bond saves a Canadian agent (played by television-show *Castle*'s Stana Katic) from falling into Quantum's hands—is reminiscent of the mission at the heart of the little-known short story "007 in New York." It's the first direct sequel in the series, picking up minutes after the end of *Casino Royale*.

Bond brings Mr. White (Jesper Christensen) in for questioning, but he is rescued by a Quantum mole inside MI6. The trail leads Bond to Haiti and businessman Dominic Greene (Mathieu Amalric), part of Quantum, who is financing a coup in Bolivia in exchange for apparently worthless rights, with the approval of the CIA. Bond follows Greene to Bregenz, where Quantum members talk at the opera; Bond eavesdrops but is blamed for the death of a Special Branch operative and disavowed. He manages to get to Bolivia, where, with the aid of local agent Camille Montes (Olga Kurylenko), as well as Felix Leiter (Jeffrey Wright, again), he learns that Quantum's plan is to control the water supply. Camille is seeking revenge on Quantum's Bolivian Army stooge General Medrano (Joaquin Cosio); she and Bond stop Quantum, killing Medrano and interrogating Greene, who is later killed by Quantum. Bond finds, but doesn't kill, the man who seduced Vesper into Quantum and is reinstated into the Secret Service.

Where *Casino Royale* was a love story, *Quantum of Solace* is all about revenge— even though Bond claims to M that he's not interested in Vesper any more (she thinks he'd be a "pretty cold bastard" if he didn't want revenge). His actions and attitude throughout the film prove differently, notably after MI6 agent Strawberry Fields

(Gemma Arterton) is killed for helping him in Bolivia. (Craig felt that Bond was "looking for revenge . . . to make himself happy with the world again.")

His relationship with M continues to be prickly, but she trusts him to get on with his job, even after she has had to suspend him from duty. He describes M to Camille as a "friend," and jokingly notes that "she likes to think" she's his mother. M is convinced Vesper loved Bond, but 007 doesn't want to hear this either from her, or later from René Mathis (Giancarlo Giannini, reprising his role from *Casino Royale*); however, eventually he concedes that she was right, which is the end of a process of his reassessing whom he can trust that occurs throughout the film. After Fields's death, M accuses him of being blinded by "inconsolable rage" and unable to distinguish his friends from his enemies, and officially suspends him from duty—but still trusts his instincts enough to let him follow the leads to Greene.

According to Greene, MI6 regards Bond as "difficult to control," and he taunts both Bond and Camille about their

OPPOSITE: *Where has the glamour gone? Empire Design depict a moment from the end of* Quantum of Solace *for the film's dramatic poster.* LEFT: *Daniel Craig and Olga Kurylenko on the opera set for* Quantum of Solace. ABOVE: *Giancarlo Giannini reprised his role as Mathis, seen here at the* Quantum of Solace *photo call.*

being "damaged goods." Apart from a brief fling with MI6 agent Fields, almost to pass the time, Bond is celibate in the film, and only exchanges a kiss with Camille at the end.

Bond's fighting prowess continues to be displayed, and he kills when he has to, regarding it as a necessary evil and not worth discussing afterwards if it's irrelevant—and now he won't be needled by M when she criticizes him for it. He will let one of the bad guys fall from a building, and isn't emotional about disposing of Mathis's body after he is killed—although he stays with the man, providing some comfort until he passes. When it seems as if all is lost, he's prepared to shoot Camille rather than let her die in a fire like her family.

He can drive a stick-shift car at high speeds while also using a semi-automatic weapon; he can ride a motorbike and knows how to fly an old Douglas DC-3 airliner, as well as handle a speedboat.

Bond continues to be charming, persuading a desk clerk to lie for him and seducing MI6 agent Fields. His main achievement is persuading Mathis to help him, despite Bond being responsible for Mathis being tortured as a possible Quantum double agent. His friendship with Felix Leiter (and the CIA agent's faith in Bond) is strong enough for Felix to pass on a lead and give Bond a heads-up when he's about to be captured, and the film concludes with Bond brought back into the fold—although as far as he's concerned, he never left.

# *SKYFALL* (2012)

There was a four-year gap before the next Bond film arrived, caused largely by MGM's financial problems. This did allow *Skyfall* to be released in the fiftieth anniversary year of the Bond film series, and for considerable polishing to be done on the script, providing what many regard as the finest 007 film yet.

*Skyfall* reunited Craig with his *Road to Perdition* director Sam Mendes, and is set some time after *Quantum of Solace* (there are no references back to the Quantum organization). Although the story is completely original, there are plenty of items drawn from Fleming, many of them relating to the character of Bond himself.

James Bond is missing, presumed killed, after an operation in Istanbul to recover a stolen hard drive containing the names of MI6 agents goes wrong and he is accidentally shot by fellow agent Eve (Naomie Harris). After a bomb explodes at MI6 headquarters,

Bond returns to duty and sets off on the trail of the thief, eventually capturing Raoul Silva, a former MI6 agent who wants revenge on M for abandoning him years earlier (Javier Bardem). Silva wanted to be captured and taken to MI6's temporary headquarters, from where he escapes and tries to kill M. Bond takes M to his boyhood home, Skyfall, in the Scottish Highlands, where he, his old gamekeeper Kincade (Albert Finney), and M battle Silva and his men. M is injured in the fight, and starts to bleed out; Silva tries to get her to shoot them both, but Bond kills him. M dies in Bond's arms; a little later, he reports for duty to Gareth Mallory, the new M (Ralph Fiennes).

Bond's relationship with M is at the heart of *Skyfall*, as we receive confirmation of some elements of the backstory alluded to in *Casino*

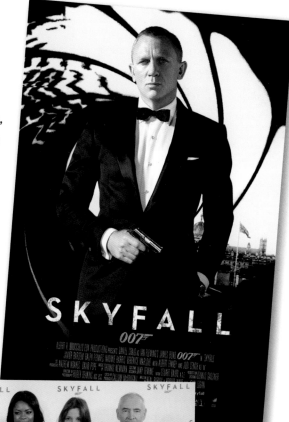

**TOP:** *The return of sophistication in Empire Design's British cinema poster for Skyfall.*
**ABOVE:** *The Skyfall team (from left to right: Javier Bardem, Bérénice Marlohe, director Sam Mendes, Dame Judi Dench, Daniel Craig, Naomie Harris, and producers Barbara Broccoli and Michael G. Wilson.*

*Royale*: Bond is an orphan, who became M's personal project years later. There have been hints at this in earlier films—M's comment about promoting him too early, Bond's quip about her thinking she's his mother—but it is now blatant. M returns him to duty even though he hasn't passed the physical; she has the typical reaction of a parent when a child who's been missing returns—relief disguised as anger—and she trusts him to look after her. Their repartee when they first ride in the Aston Martin shows the teasing relationship they now have. Silva is aware of the way M treats her agents, having been the recipient of her largesse in the past, and tries to warn Bond. This theme picks up on the paternalistic relationship between the male M of Fleming's novels and Bond, but is given a focus that Fleming would not have considered relevant.

We learn that Bond's parents, Andrew and Monique Delacroix, are "tragically departed," according to their gravestone, although no year is given; Bond was eleven at the time. He studied at public school, where homosexual advances were not unknown. He has kept his family home, Skyfall, although once he was presumed dead the contents were sold. He holds the rank of commander in the Royal Navy, and was made a Companion of the Order of St. Michael and St. George (for services unknown); the Royal Navy reference would suggest that the SAS element of his backstory suggested in *Casino Royale* is being quietly disregarded in favor of the Fleming original (members of the Navy would join the Special Boat Service rather than the SAS). His "death" warrants the head of the Service herself writing his obituary.

Even before his "death" and resurrection, Bond is more compassionate than before—he tries to help Ronson, the MI6 agent shot in Istanbul (Bill Buckhurst). However, duty comes first and he does what he has to: he knows the agent will die, so he goes after the hard drive; he returns from his island idyll after the explosion at Vauxhall Cross knowing he'll be needed. He has no compunction about destroying Skyfall—although he seems more angered when Silva's men destroy his Aston Martin!

His respect has to be earned. M has done so previously; new characters Q and Eve (later revealed to be Miss Moneypenny) manage it during the course of the film, as does the new M.

He displays more of a wry sense of humor than previously, teasing Eve about her shooting, and bantering with Q (Ben Whishaw) in a way we've not seen this Bond act previously. His stamina and confidence are both seriously affected by being shot—his swimming and gym exercises are nowhere near the level they were before, and his hand shakes when he is challenged by Silva on the villain's island—but when Silva escapes, and even more so when he realizes that M is in danger, he is able to push past all that.

He indulges in some casual sexual relationships—with a girl during his "retirement," with Eve in Shanghai, and with Silva's associate Severine (Bérénice Lim Marlohe) on the way to Silva's island—but none of them are serious (and no mention is made of Severine's death later). He enjoys his drink—whether it's a beer on the beach, whiskey, or champagne.

Timothy Dalton tried to return Bond to the character created by Ian Fleming. Daniel Craig has succeeded to a greater extent. Obviously, the details of their backgrounds are different—Fleming's Bond was a veteran of World War II; Craig's 007 saw conflict at the start of the twenty-first century—but by dramatizing *Casino Royale* as Craig's first adventure, movie audiences have seen the hard shell accrete around the character on screen as readers of the books did over half a century earlier. And, as Fleming's agent changed across the novels, so Craig's Bond has lightened to an extent (watch his reaction to the signature gun coming online in *Skyfall*, or the way he teases his old gamekeeper, Kincade). Fans of Sean Connery's approach to the role have also praised Craig's version of Bond, and it is not hard to imagine him appearing as Bond in Connery's earlier adventures.

For *SPECTRE*, his fourth film, out in the fall of 2015, Craig is working with much the same team as on *Skyfall*. Hopefully, the attention to detail in the characterization of 007 will be maintained, and Daniel Craig will show us yet more facets to Fleming's agent.

**OPPOSITE:** *Daniel Craig prepares for an action sequence on the set of Skyfall.* **RIGHT:** *Craig surrounded by friends or foes? From left to right, Naomie Harris, Lea Seydoux, Daniel Craig, Monica Bellucci, and Christoph Waltz at the SPECTRE press call.*

# THE FEMMES FATALES

*007*

Hardly a day seems to go by in the life of secret agent James Bond without someone trying to seduce him—or, at least, that's the impression you could easily come away with from the movies. From the very first film, *Dr. No*, they have been an essential part of the franchise, attractive sirens whose job it is to lure 007 away from the trail of the villain, and usually keep him occupied until someone else can finish the job. Sometimes, of course, they're perfectly capable of doing that themselves, as *GoldenEye*'s Xenia Onatopp proved!

Miss Taro (Zena Marshall), introduced in *Dr. No*, was the archetype. The secretary to Bond's contact on Jamaica, Pleydell-Smith, she is really working for SPECTRE agent Dr. No, and is instructed to bring Bond to her out-of-the-way house so he can be killed. She's surprised when 007 eludes the trap set for him, but takes the agent to bed to keep him occupied before further thugs can arrive—instead, the police arrive to arrest her (after, of course, she and Bond have slept together). Belly dancer Bonita tries the same delaying tactic at the start of *Goldfinger*, but Bond sees the image of the bad guy approaching reflected in her eyeball, and spins her round so she gets coshed instead of him.

*Actress Luciana Paluzzi plays Fiona Volpe in Thunderball.*

Fiona Volpe upped the profile of the femme fatale in *Thunderball*, acting as the mistress of NATO pilot François Derval, killing SPECTRE assassin Count Lippe, and seducing 007. Bond manages to escape her embrace and places her in the path of a bullet meant for him. The character was renamed Fatima Blush and made even more outrageous in the *Thunderball* remake, *Never Say Never Again*. She was a clear template for Helga Brandt, Mr. Osato's secretary in *You Only Live Twice*, who has her way with Bond before leaving him to die in a crashing plane—but her reward for failure is a date with Blofeld's tank of hungry piranha.

*OHMSS* was a love story at its core, and even the most desperate would find it hard to cast Blofeld's assistant Irma Bunt as a femme fatale! Willard Whyte's "playmates," Bambi and Thumper, avoid the seductive foreplay in *Diamonds Are Forever*, opting to try to beat up 007 before he turns the tables in the swimming pool. Rosie Carver in *Live and Let Die* is also far from the standard femme fatale, posing as "Mrs. Bond" to get close to the agent and set him up for Kananga's men; she runs from 007, and is killed by a Scarecrow.

Although it would seem as if Miss Anders in *The Man with the Golden Gun* fits the profile, she's actually the one who sent the bullet with 007's number to the authorities, so she's on the side of the angels even before sleeping with Bond! Karl Stromberg's assistant Naomi in *The Spy Who Loved Me* may not try to get Bond into bed, but she flirts with him during his visit to *Atlantis*—and that attitude continues throughout her attempts to kill him and Major Anya Amasova, before the KGB agent fires a missile from Bond's Lotus to destroy Naomi's helicopter.

Femmes fatales fell out of fashion in the Bond films over the next few years. The nearest that the series came during the 1980s was May Day in *A View to a Kill*, but even she does the right thing in the end, sacrificing herself to stop her lover Max Zorin's plans. However, when the series returned with *GoldenEye* in 1995, after a six-year gap, the femme fatale made a welcome reappearance with Xenia Zaragevna Onatopp, the more-than-slightly insane assistant to General Ourumov, who orgasms when she kills (and, indeed, is killed!). After a mad drive through the French mountains, she flirts with Bond before trying to seduce him—with a view to strangling him with her thighs, as she has done with others. Bond escapes, but she pursues him and Natalya Simonova to Cuba, where she ends up squeezed to death herself.

Bond's encounter with the "Cigar Girl" (the character's name was Giuletta da Vinci, according to the script, played by Maria Grazia Cucinotta) forms the pre-credit sequence of *The World Is Not Enough*, as the seductive assistant to Renard flirts with 007 before shooting his contact, and then a little later tries to kill Bond during a long chase down the Thames. Although Bond offers to protect her, she refuses to help the agent, and commits suicide rather than be captured.

Miranda Frost provides a twist on the idea of the femme fatale for the twenty-first century. Initially, it seems as if she's working for Gustav Graves in *Die Another Day*, but she's really an MI6 agent—albeit a double agent, her loyalties bought by Graves. She sleeps with Bond, but after her true allegiance is revealed she tries to kill CIA agent Jinx—only to become overconfident in her own abilities and perish.

A decade later, in *Skyfall*, Bond falls for the charms of former prostitute Severine, Raoul Silva's assistant, who spots Bond after he kills Patrice, Silva's hired assassin. She waits for him at the casino,

although she warms to Bond and warns him of an impending trap. She and 007 travel to Silva's island together, but she is used for target practice by the psychotic former agent.

With the exception of Fiona, one key thing links the characters above: none of them was created by Ian Fleming in the original 007 novels (and even Fiona came from a novel derived from a screen-play). Recognizing the place of the femme fatale in the public's expectations of Bond, however, his literary heirs did include some.

John Gardner gave us the seductive Mary Jane Mashkin in his first novel, *Licence Renewed*, and the duplicitous Heather Dare in *No Deals, Mr. Bond*; Raymond Benson provided close encounters with femmes fatales Hera Volopoulos in *The Facts of Death*, Margareta Piel in *Doubleshot*, and movie star Tylyn Mignonne in *Never Dream of Dying*; while William Boyd embraced the idea fully, making Efua Blessing Ogilvy-Grant a key character in *Solo*. Newspaper comic-strip creator Jim Lawrence added Chitra "Taj" Mahal to his adaptation of *The Man with the Golden Gun*, Nyla Larsen to "The Hildebrand Rarity," and Rona Vail to *The Spy Who Loved Me*, as well as characters such as Gretta in his original story "Trouble Spot."

It might be a role with short life-expectancy—but the femmes fatales in Bond's life certainly have fun!

*"Cigar Girl" played by Maria Grazia Cucinotta in* The World Is Not Enough.

# THE OTHER BONDS:
## THE ALTERNATIVE CASINO ROYALES

I AN FLEMING'S FIRST JAMES BOND NOVEL, *CASINO ROYALE*,
IS THE MOST FILMED STORY OF THE ENTIRE 007 CANON.
WHILE MOST PEOPLE NOWADAYS THINK OF DANIEL CRAIG'S
DEBUT APPEARANCE, THERE WERE TWO PREVIOUS VERSIONS
OF THE TALE, BOTH WITH THEIR OWN VERY DISTINCTIVE
INTERPRETATIONS OF THE BRITISH SECRET SERVICE'S TOP AGENT.

The first of these appeared on October 21, 1954, not on
the big screen, but as an hour of live American television. CBS-TV's *Climax!* anthology series was home to
Barry Nelson's portrayal of "Card Sharp" Jimmy Bond;
the mystery show ran for four seasons, and included versions of many classic thrillers, including Raymond Chandler's *The Long Goodbye*.

While the idea of an American James Bond may be
anathema to some—and remember, on at least two occasions, with John Gavin and Burt Reynolds, the official
series flirted with casting someone from the other side

**OPPOSITE:** *Peter Lorre as Le Chiffre (far right) and Barry Nelson (far left) in
the very first screen appearance of Ian Fleming's secret agent, the CBS Climax!
adaptation of Casino Royale in 1954.* **RIGHT:** *Barry Nelson, who played "Card
Sharp" Jimmy Bond on TV in 1954.*

of the Atlantic—the majority of the adaptation was faithful to the core of Fleming's story, with Bond ordered to beat Le Chiffre at baccarat, and ending up being tortured by the villain to hand over the winnings. The most noticeable thing to change was the nationality of the participants.

There were, of course, quite a few differences in the character. Jimmy Bond (never "James," and certainly not 007) works for the Combined Intelligence Agency, and is briefed by British Secret Service agent Clarence Leiter. He's an expert card player—who gained the nickname "Card Sharp Jimmy Bond" when playing against a Maharajah at Deauville—and he has the same eye for the ladies as his British counterpart (the characters of Vesper Lynd and René Mathis are combined into Valerie Mathis, a Deuxième Bureau agent who's one of Bond's former lovers). He's not as elegant as the later screen Bonds—the crew cut doesn't go particularly well with the tuxedo, although Fleming's Bond sported a crew cut in *Live and Let Die*—and often seems to be more of a hard-boiled detective than a secret agent.

"JAMES BOND"    25-

REEL ONE A         "CASINO ROYALE"      DIALOGUE CONTINUITY
yj  4-21-67            PROD. #8778              PAGE 1

Children:    (SINGING IN FRENCH) "FRERE JACQUES"

Inspector Mathis:Mister Bond?

Evelyn:      Yes?

Inspector Mathis:I'm Lieutenant Mathis, of the Special Police.

Children:    (SINGING)

Inspector Mathis:These are my credentials.

Evelyn:      They appear to be in order.

Inspector Mathis:Come with me.

McTarry:     They used to say a good spy is a pure spy, inside and
             Roses, Tanagra figurines and Debussy. He plays Debu
             every afternoon, from unset until it's too dark to r
             the music. Stands on his head a lot. Eats Royal Je
             Lets his intestines down and washes them by hand. S
             thing he learned during his sojourn in Tibet.

Ransome:     Them? What gives?

McTarry:     I forgot to mention lions.

Smernov:     Lions and more lions.

Ransome:     We're surrounded by lions.

Smernov:     I did not come here to be devoured by symbols of m

Le Grand:    I warn you M, if this is a trap....

McTarry:     Calm yourselves, gentlemen. It's no trap, I assur
             The lions are only curious. He has few visitors.

Le Grand:    That I can believe.

McTarry:     A variable Eden, is it not, gentlemen?

Le Grand:    Eden without any Eve is an absurdity.

Ransome:     A good spy is a pure spy.

Le Grand:    Not good...great. The greatest spy in history, gen

McTarry:     The true, one and only, original - James Bond.

Bond's servant:The gentlemen are here, Sir James.

Bond:        Thank you.

McTarry:     My dear Bond.

Bond:        My dear M.

Ransome:     Ransome, C.I.A., Sir James.

Bond:        Uh - J-J-Junior Cypher c-c-clerk in my day, weren't you
             Ransome?

RED JUN 2 1967

TELEPHONE 816-561-3031                              CABLE ADDRESS — COLUMFILM

COLUMBIA PICTURES
C O R P O R A T I O N
3130 BROADWAY              KANSAS CITY, MISSOURI 64111

Bond:    Oh. Why are the two flags here in the Carribean?
Hardley: We've been out of contact for a month, sir...we're not sure which one to
         leave.
Bond:    Who's there?
Hardley: Your nephew, air - uh - Jimmy Bond.
Bond:    Oh. Rather a disappointment, I'm afraid, little Jimmy.
Jimmy Bond: Listen, you can't shoot me. I - I - I - I have a very low threshold of
         death. Uh - my doctor says I cannot let bullets enter my body
         at - at any time. I - I -

ADDRESS ALL COMMUNICATIONS TO THE COMPANY

**OPPOSITE:** *Robert McGinnis's psychedelic art for the justly-maligned 1967 comedy adaptation of Casino Royale.* **LEFT:** *Two pages of dialogue from one of the many dozens of different scripts prepared for Casino Royale.*

Jimmy is able to resist torture—in this case, a pair of pliers being applied to his toes rather than the genital-beating of the original; unsurprisingly, CBS ensured writers Anthony Ellis and Charles Bennet toned down Fleming's grotesque scene. He's closer to the Dalton or Craig versions of Bond in his ability to absorb punishment but still show a degree of vulnerability. "I'm no hero . . . I don't like pain," he explains to Peter Lorre's Le Chiffre.

There was a vague possibility of further Jimmy Bond adventures, but nothing materialized; Fleming was asked by CBS to pitch further stories in 1958—these formed the core of the short-story collection *For Your Eyes Only*, and Anthony Horowitz's *Trigger Mortis*.

However, because of this early sale, the rights to *Casino Royale* weren't available to EON for a long time, and this allowed a rival version of Bond to arrive in cinemas in 1967, battling for supremacy with Sean Connery's *You Only Live Twice*.

If you simply look at the credits for the 1967 *Casino Royale*, you can start to see why the film is such a mess. Five directors are billed, and there's at least one (Richard Talmadge) who didn't receive official credit. Stars Woody Allen and Peter Sellers rewrote sections of Wolf Mankowitz, John Law, and Michael Sayers's script, as did director Val Guest, and writers Joseph Heller, Terry Southern, and Billy Wilder. A straightforward adaptation had been scripted some years earlier by Academy Award–winner Ben Hecht, but this was reworked long before the cameras began turning.

"*Casino Royale* is too much . . . for one James Bond!" ran the tagline on the poster, and there are indeed multiple versions of Bond in the film. The primary one is David Niven's Sir James Bond, a retired agent of the British Secret Service, called upon (and then forced) to help defeat SMERSH one last time. Appropriately enough, given that Niven had been Fleming's own pick to play the agent, this is per-

*Peter Sellers and Ursula Andress prepare for their strenuous days filming the 1967 version of* Casino Royale.

haps the most serious of the incarnations seen in the film: Sir James had won the Victoria Cross at the Siege of Mafeking, and was a hero of the Ashanti Uprising. He had a daughter by his lover, Mata Hari, before he was forced to lure her across the frontier into France, where she was executed. He is an accomplished pianist, eats royal jelly to keep young, grows black roses, and drives a vintage Bentley. He's an excellent shot. His name and designation have been passed on to other agents to keep the legend of 007 alive, with Sir James sniffily referring to the "sexual acrobat who leaves a trail of beautiful dead women behind like blown roses," and after the death of M, he takes over as head of the Secret Service. There's something of the mature Bond that Connery went on to play in *Never Say Never Again* about Niven's Sir James: a man who has done what was necessary in the past, and now wants to enjoy the fruits of his retirement.

*Woody Allen as Jimmy Bond, one of the many stars of the spoof version of Fleming's original story.*

To confuse SMERSH—and the audience—nearly everyone else in the movie, it seems, becomes known as James Bond at some point or other. Most importantly, Peter Sellers's card-playing genius Evelyn Tremble adopts the name for his important baccarat game against Orson Welles's Le Chiffre. Woody Allen's Dr. Noah is really Jimmy Bond, Sir James's nephew, who is in charge of SMERSH; he has rather a large number of insane plans, ranging from releasing robot doubles of Sir James to cause devastation and letting loose a bacillus that makes all women beautiful and kills all men taller than 4 foot 6 inches, to developing a pill that turns people into walking atomic bombs. It's this last which proves fatal for everyone named Bond in the film, after Jimmy is forced to swallow one of them, and blows himself, and everyone else, up.

*Casino Royale* is spectacularly unfunny, despite the presence of so much talent—Sellers, at the height of his fame, wanted to play his part seriously and was unhappy with many aspects of the production. After he failed to complete shooting, the movie had to be cut around what he had filmed. It would be another thirty years before a Bond parody was nailed, with Mike Myers's *Austin Powers: International Man of Mystery* . . .

# AFTERWORD:
## THE ESSENTIAL BOND

During the seven decades so far that James Bond has appeared in popular culture, he has been written by many different authors, but, with the notable (and deliberate) exception of the 1967 *Casino Royale* movie, he has remained recognizably the same character that Ian Fleming created when he sat down behind his typewriter in the study of his home in Jamaica.

"James Bond has become encrusted with mannerisms and belongings and individual characteristics," Fleming explained toward the end of his life. "This is probably a natural outgrowth of getting to know him better. I don't know if this is good or bad, and I don't know where all the elements that compose Bond come from, but there they are."

Even the worst excesses of the Roger Moore era—*Moonraker*'s parade around St. Mark's Square, Venice, in a motorized gondola probably being the absolute nadir of any Bond story for

*Ian Fleming's Royal Quiet Deluxe Portable gold-plated typewriter, which he bought himself as a present for finishing* Casino Royale.

fans of the character—retained many of Bond's core characteristics: his enjoyment of good food and drink; his love of the ladies; his willingness to do whatever it takes; and, above all, his staunch patriotism. Whether played by a Scot, an Australian, an Englishman, a Welshman, or an Irishman, his loyalty is to the Crown and to his country, and woe betide anyone who gets in his way!

The last word on 007 should go to Fleming himself: "Bond is not a hero, nor is he depicted as being very likable or admirable. He is a Secret Service agent. He's not a bad man, but he is ruthless and self-indulgent. He enjoys the fight; he also enjoys the prizes."

# JAMES BOND BIBLIOGRAPHY

**The adventures of 007 in print (by chronological order of release)**

*Casino Royale* (novel, Ian Fleming, 1953)

*Live and Let Die* (novel, Ian Fleming, 1954)

*Moonraker* (novel, Ian Fleming, 1955)

*Diamonds Are Forever* (novel, Ian Fleming, 1956)

*From Russia, with Love* (novel, Ian Fleming, 1957)

*Dr. No* (novel, Ian Fleming, 1958)

*Goldfinger* (novel, Ian Fleming, 1959)

*For Your Eyes Only* (short story collection: "From a View to a Kill"; "For Your Eyes Only"; "Quantum of Solace"; "Risico"; "The Hildebrand Rarity": Ian Fleming, 1960)

*Thunderball* (novel, Ian Fleming, 1961)

"The Living Daylights" (short story, Ian Fleming, 1962)

*The Spy Who Loved Me* (novel, Ian Fleming, 1962)

*On Her Majesty's Secret Service* (novel, Ian Fleming, 1963)

"007 in New York" (short story, Ian Fleming, 1963)

"Property of a Lady" (short story, Ian Fleming, 1963)

*You Only Live Twice* (novel, Ian Fleming, 1964)

*The Man with the Golden Gun* (novel, Ian Fleming, 1965)

*Octopussy* (short story collection originally comprising "Octopussy" and "The Living Daylights," Ian Fleming, 1966)

*The Adventures of James Bond Junior 003½* (children's novel, R.D. Mascott, 1967)

*Colonel Sun* (novel, 'Robert Markham' [Kingsley Amis], 1968)

*James Bond: The Authorized Biography* (novel, John Pearson, 1973)

*James Bond, The Spy Who Loved Me* (novel, Christopher Wood, 1977)

*Licence Renewed* (novel, John Gardner, 1981)

*For Special Services* (novel, John Gardner, 1982)

*Icebreaker* (novel, John Gardner, 1983)

*Role of Honor* (novel, John Gardner, 1984)

*Nobody Lives for Ever* (novel, John Gardner, 1986)

*No Deals, Mr. Bond* (novel, John Gardner, 1987)

*Scorpius* (novel, John Gardner, 1988)

*Win, Lose or Die* (novel, John Gardner, 1989)

*Brokenclaw* (novel, John Gardner, 1990)

*The Man from Barbarossa* (novel, John Gardner, 1991)

*Death is Forever* (novel, John Gardner, 1992)

*Never Send Flowers* (novel, John Gardner, 1993)

*Seafire* (novel, John Gardner, 1994)

*COLD* (novel, John Gardner, 1996)

"Blast from the Past" (short story, Raymond Benson, 1997)

*Zero Minus Ten* (novel, Raymond Benson, 1997)

*The Facts of Death* (novel, Raymond Benson, 1998)

"Midsummer's Night Doom" (short story, Raymond Benson, 1999)

*High Time to Kill* (novel, Raymond Benson, 1999)

"Live at Five" (short story, Raymond Benson, 1999)

*Doubleshot* (novel, Raymond Benson, 2000)

*Never Dream of Dying* (novel, Raymond Benson, 2001)

*The Man with the Red Tattoo* (novel, Raymond Benson, 2002)

*SilverFin* (Young Bond, Charlie Higson, 2005)

*The Moneypenny Diaries: Guardian Angel* (novel, "Kate Westbrook" [Samantha Weinberg], 2005)

*Blood Fever* (Young Bond, Charlie Higson, 2006)

*Secret Servant: The Moneypenny Diaries* (novel, "Kate Westbrook" [Samantha Weinberg], 2006)

*Double or Die* (Young Bond, Charlie Higson, 2007)

*Hurricane Gold* (Young Bond, Charlie Higson, 2007)

*The Moneypenny Diaries: Final Fling* (novel, "Kate Westbrook" [Samantha Weinberg], 2008)

*Devil May Care* (novel, Sebastian Faulks, 2008)

*By Royal Command* (Young Bond, Charlie Higson, 2008)

"A Hard Man to Kill" (Young Bond short story, Charlie Higson, 2009)

*Carte Blanche* (novel, Jeffery Deaver, 2011)

*Solo* (novel, William Boyd, 2013)

*Shoot to Kill* (Young Bond, Steve Cole, 2014)

*Trigger Mortis* (novel, Anthony Horowitz, 2015)

# JAMES BOND FILMOGRAPHY

**The adventures of 007 on screen (by chronological order of release)**

*Casino Royale* (TV, Barry Nelson, 1954)

*Dr. No* (movie, Sean Connery, 1962)

*From Russia with Love* (movie, Sean Connery, 1963)

*Goldfinger* (movie, Sean Connery, 1964)

*Thunderball* (movie, Sean Connery, 1965)

*Casino Royale* (movie, David Niven/Peter Sellers, 1967)

*You Only Live Twice* (movie, Sean Connery, 1967)

*On Her Majesty's Secret Service* (movie, George Lazenby, 1969)

*Diamonds Are Forever* (movie, Sean Connery, 1971)

*Live and Let Die* (movie, Roger Moore, 1973)

*The Man with the Golden Gun* (movie, Roger Moore, 1974)

*The Spy Who Loved Me* (movie, Roger Moore, 1977)

*Moonraker* (movie, Roger Moore, 1979—novelized by Christopher Wood as James Bond and Moonraker)

*For Your Eyes Only* (movie, Roger Moore, 1981)

*Octopussy* (movie, Roger Moore, 1983)

*Never Say Never Again* (movie, Sean Connery, 1983)

*A View to a Kill* (movie, Roger Moore, 1985)

*The Living Daylights* (movie, Timothy Dalton, 1987)

*GoldenEye* (movie, Pierce Brosnan, 1995—novelized by John Gardner)

*Licence to Kill* (movie, Timothy Dalton, 1989—novelized by John Gardner)

*Tomorrow Never Dies* (movie, Pierce Brosnan, 1997—novelized by Raymond Benson)

*The World Is Not Enough* (movie, Pierce Brosnan, 1999—novelized by Raymond Benson)

*Die Another Day* (movie, Pierce Brosnan, 2002—novelized by Raymond Benson)

*Casino Royale* (movie, Daniel Craig, 2006)

*Quantum of Solace* (movie, Daniel Craig, 2008)

*Skyfall* (movie, Daniel Craig, 2012)

*SPECTRE* (movie, Daniel Craig, 2015)

# PHOTOGRAPHY CREDITS

**4. The Other Literary Bonds: From Robert Markham to Anthony Horowitz**

p.48: © Rolls Press/Popperfoto/Getty Images

p.59: © Julien's Auctions

p.62: © Vipin Kumar/Hindustan Times/Getty Images

p.63: © Rex Features/REX USA

p.64: © Leon Neal/AFP/Getty Images

p.65: © David Levenson/Getty Images

p.68: © J. Vespa/WireImage/Getty Images

**Sidebar: The Guns**

p.69: © Julien's Auctions

p.70: © William Thomas Cain/Getty Images

p.71, left: © Ray Tang/Rex/REX USA

p.71, right: © Jonathan Hordle/REX USA

**5. Sean Connery: The Scottish Bond**

p.72: © AFP/Getty Images

p.73: © PPR/Rex/REX USA

p.76: top, middle & bottom © Julien's Auctions

p.77: © Ray Fisher/The LIFE Images Collection/Getty Images

p.78: bottom left & right © Julien's Auctions

p.79, top: © Harry Myers/REX USA

p.79, bottom: © Chris Ware/Getty Images

p.80: © Julien's Auctions

p.81: right © Julien's Auctions

p.82, left: © Paul Popper/Popperfoto/Getty Images

p.82, right: © Popperfoto/Getty Images

p.83, top: © Harry Myers/REX USA

p.83, bottom: © REX USA

p.84: top, middle & bottom © Julien's Auctions

p.85, bottom: © Mondadori Portfolio/Getty Images

p.86: © Popperfoto/Getty Images

p.87, top left: © Beverley Goodway/Daily Mail/REX USA

p.87, top right: © Daily Mail/REX USA

p.87, bottom right: © Julien's Auctions

p.88, bottom: © Chris Jackson/Getty Images

p.89, top: © Mondadori Portfolio via Getty Images

p.89, bottom: © Keystone-France/Gamma-Keystone/Getty Images

p.91: top, middle & bottom left © Julien's Auctions

p.92, top: © Terry O'Neill/Getty Images

p.92, bottom: © Anwar Hussein/Getty Images

p.93: © Anwar Hussein/Getty Images

**6. George Lazenby: The Australian Bond**

p.96: © Manchester Daily Express/Getty Images

p.97: © Daily Mail/REX USA

p.98: right © Julien's Auctions

p.99, top: © Larry Ellis Collection/Getty Images

p.99, middle: © Phillip Jackson/Associated Newspapers/Rex/REX USA

p.99, bottom: © Phillip Jackson/Daily Mail/Rex/REX USA

p.100, top: © Phillip Jackson/Daily Mail/REX USA

p.100, bottom: © Harry Myers/REX USA

**Sidebar: The Bond Girls**

p.101, top: © Hulton Archive/Getty Images

p.101, bottom: © Anwar Hussein/Getty Images

p.102: © Mirco Toniolo/REX USA

p.103: © Kent Gavin/Keystone/Getty Images

**7. Roger Moore: The Urbane Bond**

p.104: © Peter Ruck/BIPs/Getty Images

p.105: © Roger Garwood/Associated Newspapers/Rex/REX USA

p.107, middle & bottom: © Julien's Auctions

p.108, top: © Terry O'Neill/Hulton Archive/Getty Images

p.108, bottom: © Popperfoto/Getty Images

p.109, top: © Hulton Archive/Getty Images

p.109, bottom: © Harry Myers/REX USA

p.111: © Monitor Picture Library/Photoshot/Getty Images

p.113: top & bottom right © Julien's Auctions

p.114: © Harry Myers/REX USA

p.115: © Michael Fresco/Daily Mail/REX USA

p.116, bottom: © Harry Myers/REX USA

p.117: © Harry Myers/REX USA

p.118, top & bottom right: © Julien's Auctions

p.119, left: © Keith Hamshere/Getty Images

p.119, right: © Keith Hamshere/Getty Images

p.120: © Keith Hamshere/Getty Images

p.121, bottom: © Bryn Colton/Getty Images

p.123, top: © United News/Popperfoto/Getty Images

p.123, bottom: © Chris Barham/Associated Newspapers/Rex/REX USA

**Sidebar: Rebooting Bond**

p.124: © SN/Rex/REX USA

p.125: © Gareth Cattermole/Getty Images

**8. Timothy Dalton: The Bleeding Bond**

p.126: © Larry Ellis Collection/Getty Images

p.128, top: © Harry Myers/REX USA

p.128, bottom: © Graham Trott/Daily Mail/Rex/REX USA

p.130, top: © Nils Jorgensen/REX USA

p.130, bottom: © Julien's Auctions

p.131: © Nils Jorgensen/REX USA

p.132, bottom: © Julien's Auctions

p.133, top: © George Rose/Getty Images

p.133, bottom: © Georges De Keerle/Getty Images

**Sidebar: The Music of James Bond**

p.135, right: © Dave Hogan/Getty Images

p.136, top: © Express/Getty Images

p.137: © Harry Myers/REX USA

p.138: © Express/Archive Photos/Getty Images

p.139: © Ron Galella/WireImage/Getty Images

p.140: © Dave Hogan/Getty Images

p.141: © Jason Merritt/Getty Images

9. Pierce Brosnan: The Irish Bond

p.142: © Keith Hamshere/Getty Images

p.145, top: © Keith Hamshere/Getty Images

p.145, bottom: © Keith Hamshere/Getty Images

p.146: © Dave Benett/Getty Images

p.148: © Peter Bischoff/Getty Images

p.149, bottom: © Eric Vandeville/Gamma-Rapho/Getty Images

p.150, right: © Ken McKay/REX USA

p.150, left: © REX USA

p.152, top: © Nils Jorgensen/REX USA

p.152, middle: © Nick Robinson/REX USA

p.152, bottom: © Julien's Auctions

p.154: © Richard Young/REX USA

**Sidebar: The Villains**

p.155: © Express Newspapers/Hulton Archive/Getty Images

p.156: © Nils Jorgensen/REX USA

p.157: © Serge Benhamou/Gamma-Rapho/Getty Images

**10. Daniel Craig: The Blond Bond**

p.158: © Gareth Cattermole

p.160: © Dave Hogan/Getty Images

p.162: © Scott Myers/REX USA

p.163: © Norbert Kesten/REX USA

p.165, top: © B 53/AFP/Getty Images

p.165, bottom: © REX USA

p.167, right: © Maria Laura Antonelli/REX USA

p.167, left: © Handout/Getty Images

p.169, bottom: Murray Sanders / Daily Mail/Rex/REX USA

p.170: © Bauer-Griffin/GC Images/Getty Images

p.171: © Mike Marsland/WireImage/Getty Images

**Sidebar: The Femmes Fatales**

p.172: © Rolls Press/Popperfoto/Getty Images

p.173: © Keith Hamshere/MoviePix/Getty Images

**11. The Other Bonds: The Alternate Casino Royales**

p.174: © CBS Photo Archive/Getty Images

p.175: © Everett Collection/REX USA

p.177: left & right © Julien's Auctions

p.178: © Terry O'Neill/Getty Images

p.179: © Terry O'Neill/Getty Images

**Afterword: The Essential Bond**

p.181: © Tim Rooke/REX USA

# INDEX

# ACKNOWLEDGMENTS

Thanks to everyone who has assisted with this latest foray into the murky worlds of James Bond, especially to:

My editor, Jeannine Dillon at Race Point Publishing, for pursuing this project through to commissioning it, and for helping to shape it into a different sort of book about 007, and Steve Burdett for saving me from some unforced errors—any that remain are strictly my responsibility! Beta-readers Brian J. Robb and Scott Harrison, who were able to suggest ways that the full picture could be covered in the format.

Iain Coupar, Caitlin Fultz, Erik Gilg, Lee Harris, Emlyn Rees, Amanda Rutter, Kathleen Spinelli, Susan Hogan, Tracy Stanley, Madeleine Vassaly, and David Thomas Moore for helping to keep the wheels of commerce moving.

Monica Derwent, Sophie Parsons, Patricia Hyde, Eve Woodlands, and Adina Mihaela Roman for technical advice.

All the Right Notes choir and the Hurst Singers for the anticipated musical diversions, and Mike Wood and the Burgess Hill Choral Society for the unexpected ones!

The staff of the Hassocks branch of the West Sussex Libraries service, who once again assisted with tracking down rare items, and exemplified why we need library service to continue.

My partner, Barbara, and my daughter, Sophie, for their love and support, even when I'm getting frazzled, and our terriers, Rani and Rodo, who give the phrase "undercover" a whole different meaning.

# ABOUT THE AUTHOR

Paul Simpson has been a fan of 007 for over forty years, and previously co-authored *The Bond Files* as well as contributed essays to Titan Publishing's reprints of the Bond newspaper strips.

He is the author of over two dozen non-fiction books, including *Middle-earth Envisioned* (Race Point Publishing) and conspiracy overview *That's What They Want You to Think* (Zenith Press), as well as guides on the works of C.S. Lewis, L. Frank Baum, and Stephen King. His most recent book is *A Brief Guide to the Sound of Music* (Running Press).

He lives in the south of England where he is the managing editor of the genre website Sci-Fi Bulletin.